SMOKE SIGNALS FROM SAMARCAND

FOR MY MOTHER

Maralin Payne Bennett

SMOKE SIGNALS
FROM SAMARCAND

The 1931 Reform School Fire and its Aftermath

BARBARA BENNETT

The University of South Carolina Press

Published by the University of South Carolina Press
Columbia, South Carolina 29208

www.sc.edu/uscpress

Manufactured in the United States of America

27 26 25 24 23 22 21 20 19 18
10 9 8 7 6 5 4 3 2 1

The Library of Congress Cataloging-in-Publication Data
can be found at http://catalog.loc.gov/.

ISBN 978-1-61117-860-9 (cloth)
ISBN 978-1-61117-861-6 (ebook)

This book was printed on recycled paper with
30 percent postconsumer waste content.

Much Madness is divinest Sense –
To a discerning Eye –
Much Sense – the starkest Madness –
'Tis the Majority
In this, as all, prevail –
Assent – and you are sane –
Demur – you're straightway dangerous –
And handled with a Chain –

Emily Dickinson

Contents

Illustrations

Acknowledgments

Many thanks go to Mona Sinquefield for her stellar research in the archives of North Carolina. I could not have finished this book without her preliminary work that saved me hours and hours of time. Also thanks to Lee Smith for her encouragement. Fred Hobson read my early drafts tirelessly and made significant suggestions that improved the manuscript, and he did so without complaint. I want to thank my friends Susan Irons, Jill McCorkle, and Marianne Gingher for our time together that kept me inspired. And always, thanks to my dogs, Milo and Sam, for keeping me sane and reminding me that a good walk can clear my head and make me a better writer.

Source material throughout this volume is taken mainly from the Nell Battle Lewis papers in the State Archives of North Carolina in Raleigh. This includes letters, interviews, personal notes, and newspaper articles.

PROLOGUE

Fire

On the evening of March 12, 1931, at Samarcand Manor Training School for Delinquent Girls just outside of Carthage, North Carolina, in the sand hills, a thin stream of smoke rose slowly from the roof near the chimney on the second floor of Bickett Hall. None of the girls eating dinner in Tufts Hall noticed it—or at least they pretended not to notice it. Gradually the smoke thickened, turning blacker as the plume rose to the sky that was slowly turning to night. Several of the girls and a few of the matrons looked up from their biscuits and stew to sniff the air suspiciously, but still no one mentioned the smell of burning. Perhaps they assumed that it came from the nearby kitchen building.

Fifteen-year-old Pearl Stiles slipped into the dining room quietly and took a seat between Margaret Abernethy and Marian Mercer. No words passed between them, but subtle smiles and lifted eyebrows punctuated their silence.

Mrs. Moore, who monitored the girls during their dinners, warned Pearl about being late and that punishment would ensue if she were late again. Pearl dipped her head in deference to Mrs. Moore's warning, and the girls around her stifled giggles. The girls near Pearl seemed distracted, finding it difficult to focus on their dinners. A few glanced toward the windows, made wavy by old glass.

One of the girls, Betty Robinson was in her nightgown when she dashed down the stairs that led to her bedroom on the second floor, where she had been resting. She had a look of panic on her pale and sickly face and began yelling about fire and smoke coming from Bickett Hall.

Two hundred girls left their long tables by lifting their skirts and swinging their legs over the benches. They rushed to the windows along with Mrs.

Moore, Miss Markham, Miss McClary, Miss Carver, and Miss Woods, who had been sitting at the teachers' table. They strained their necks, trying to see around the corner of their own building to Bickett, which was set in the midst of pine trees and sandy hills. Then, like a school of fish swimming in unison, they all moved from the windows to the front hall and out into the yard, where a clearer view of Bickett was available. What they saw set them all to chattering and jumping up and down: flames were flicking out the edges of the windows of the second story, and dark smoke plumed from the shingles of the roof like fog off a dark bog. The fire had spread so fast that the crackling of flames could already be heard above the excited prattle of the girls.

Mrs. Moore warned the girls back, stretching out her arms to the sides and herding them away from Bickett. The other teachers, mostly young and as stricken with the scene as the girls they were charged with monitoring, seemed frozen in place, so Mrs. Moore again took the lead and began ringing the dinner bell that hung from the porch rafters of Tufts Hall. Glancing over her shoulder occasionally to watch the progress of the fire, she continued to ring the bell furiously, as if she could fight the flames by the sheer force of her movement.

Other teachers, administrators, and straggling girls began to appear from various buildings at Samarcand, where they had been finishing lessons or completing household chores. More bells rang, and staff members began forming a line to throw buckets of water on the fire while others uselessly sprayed garden hoses on what had quickly become an out-of-control blaze. From somewhere in the distance they heard a siren, firemen called by Miss Agnes MacNaughton, the school superintendent, but it would be too late. Bickett Hall and all of its furnishings, including the girls' meager possessions in the dormitory rooms, would burn to the ground before the firemen could set up their hoses. By the time water streamed, its purpose was merely to douse the final sparks and keep the surrounding trees and buildings from catching fire from a stray ember. All that was left of Bickett Hall was part of the framing, the fireplaces, and some dark, indistinguishable lumps, wet and mushy in piles of soot.

While firemen continued to shoot water on the dying coals, girls began to whisper to each other, wondering what the consequences of this fire would be and if those who had been housed in Bickett would be sent home. In the midst of all this guessing and expectation, four girls found the opportunity to slip out of the crowd and move toward their own dormitory, Chamberlain Hall, without being seen by the distracted matrons. Margaret

Abernethy, Ollie Harding, Marian Mercer, and Thelma Council entered the hall and walked up the stairs to the second floor, formulating a plan while they walked. With Marian holding a cotton stocking hanging straight down, Margaret lit a match to it and then stuffed the stocking in a hole near the ceiling, fanning the flames gently to keep them alive. She then shoved the burning stocking through to the other side of the hole, into the attic. The girls knew that the space was filled with dry boxes of papers and books, old wooden toys, and cartons of rotting clothing. It would not take long for the fire to catch. They then moved soundlessly down the stairs and out the door to join the other girls, who were still staring in wonder at the ruins of Bickett.

Fifteen minutes later one fireman shouted, "Fire!" and pointed to wisps of smoke coming from the attic vent in Chamberlain. Several firemen followed him as he sprinted into the house and up the stairs. Ten minutes later they returned, their faces stern and full of anger. By now Sheriff C. J. McDonald had arrived, and the firemen reported directly to him. The men discussed among themselves whether these fires were related and seemed sure that arson was involved.

All this time Mrs. Moore had been scanning the crowd of girls, looking for Pearl Stiles, and when she found her talking to Margaret Abernethy and Marian Mercer, she pursed her lips and narrowed her eyes. She was suspicious. All three girls were incorrigible, disobedient, and generally bad to the core in her opinion, but still, she had no real proof. She decided to share her thoughts with Miss MacNaughton in the morning rather than try to get her attention in the chaos of the moment. She kept her eyes on the girls.

By now the sky had grown completely dark and the temperature was dropping in the early spring night, so the girls were herded back into their individual cottages, fifty or so to a building. In Chamberlain, though, there were only thirty because it was the discipline hall, and girls moved in and out of the building as their behavior warranted. The girls normally housed in Bickett were distributed among the other, already-overcrowded dorms, and everyone tried to settle down for the night despite the dramatic events around them. As the girls entered Chamberlain, rumors spread in whispers about another fire, this one burning the place down so there would be nowhere to house the girls and they would all have to be sent home. It was hard to tell what was a plan and what was just rumor. Every girl looked guilty just for listening to the stories.

Mrs. Moore and the other teachers staying in Chamberlain assisted with directing girls to their individual dorm rooms to get ready for bed. Miss McClary was responsible for locking certain girls in their rooms—girls who were potential runaways and therefore were held prisoner each night. First she locked in roommates Rosa Mull and Wilma Owens, and then she locked in Edna Clark, Dolores Seawell, and finally Josephine French, who had dawdled in the hall until Miss McClary grabbed her by the arm and forced her into her bedroom. Some of the rooms, such as Josephine's, did not have cots, and there the girls were made to sleep on single blankets on the hard floors. The bedbugs and cockroaches were annoying in this building, especially if a girl had to sleep on the floor, and girls in those circumstances were always complaining about not being able to get any sleep with all the insects. Tonight, though, they paid less attention to the vermin and more to the rumors of fires to come.

One by one the lamps were extinguished, and all that could be heard was the final preparations for bed being made by the matrons and teachers in the house. Then, finally, all was still.

Outside, the firemen had done all they could in the darkness, and they had sped away on the dirt roads past farms and homes, over the railroad tracks, and back toward the county seat of Carthage. The sheriff and several of his men had left Samarcand too, promising to return the next day to investigate the fires. All that remained of Bickett was the smell of smoke, piles of charred wood, and blackened fireplace bricks creating stark silhouettes against the light of the rising moon.

Back in Chamberlain, Margaret Pridgen, who had been at Samarcand Manor for twenty-one months and had no idea how much longer she would be held there, decided to take her fate into her own hands once and for all. She was scheduled for a whipping the next day for being rude to a teacher, so she figured it might as well be tonight that she made something happen. It would not be her first whipping, and she knew the drill of removing her outer clothes, lying down on the floor face down, and having Miss Stott lash her more than a hundred times with a hickory stick while Miss MacNaughton and several other teachers witnessed her humiliation. She had been sent to the infirmary one time before, bleeding and bruised from the ordeal, and she was not about to subject herself to that again. Better now than tomorrow night to make her move, since she might be too weak and sore to do anything for days.

Silently she opened her closet and touched her flimsy flowered dress, so thin and worn she could almost see through the cloth. It was the only one she had other than the blue uniform she had to wear daily. She flicked out a match from the box she kept hidden to light her illegal cigarettes, struck it, and ran the flame slowly along the hem of the dress. Once it caught, she closed the door of the closet and waited, and then she opened it again to make sure it was still going and growing larger. When she saw that the fire was burning steadily and that the wood of the closet was bound to catch, she closed the door and moved toward the hallway.

In three separate bedrooms in Chamberlain this act was repeated, and four blazes were started at nearly the same time, around 9:15. Margaret Abernethy, in her bed, smelled smoke and got up to open her bedroom door. The halls were already filling with smoke, and she moved quietly down the stairs to the first floor and toward the front door of the dorm. Other figures, shadowy and unidentifiable in their pale nightgowns, followed her. Suddenly a cry sounded from one of the rooms: "Fire! Fire! Fire!" Girls jumped out of bed, ran to the hall, and realized that smoke was coming not just from one spot but from four. Some of the girls who had not lit fires panicked, but most handled the crisis as though they were used to expecting the worst in life.

Josephine French, locked in her room, began to pound on her door and shout to be let out, and her plea was echoed by the other girls in the same situation. Hilda Godley ran through the smoke to Miss McClary's room and begged for the keys to the locked dorm rooms, but Miss McClary refused, ready to wait it out and see how serious it was. Without arguing—and simply as a decision she knew she could make—Hilda ran back to Josephine's room and popped the lock open with a spoon she had been hiding in her sleeve for just such a time as this. Opening a locked door in Chamberlain was something nearly all the girls knew how to do. When Miss McClary saw that letting the girls out was inevitable and probably a good idea, she reluctantly handed her keys to Hilda and then headed downstairs and out into the yard.

Once again girls poured from Chamberlain, this time under a clear full moon, pushing and shoving each other to get out first, cursing like many had heard their fathers do, and laughing and joking at more high excitement in one night. Eventually girls from the other dorms joined them in the excitement of the seemingly never-ending night of flames.

Miss Stott had immediately phoned the fire station when she heard the cries, but she was informed that the firemen had not returned from their first trip to Samarcand. They would first have to arrive in Carthage before they could be told to return to the school for yet another fire. There was nothing to do but wait.

Meanwhile, Chamberlain had blossomed into a spectacular fire, flames leaping out windows and licking the sides of the building like eager tongues.

Occasionally a window would explode out and a burst of smoke would billow upward. The heat of this newest inferno drove the girls and women back as the fire continued to grow and leap toward the sky. As the girls watched, their eyes glinted in the night, reflecting the heat and passion of the flames. Their faces showed more emotion than they usually allowed themselves to display in this severe setting of Samarcand. A spontaneous cheer went up as the roof caved in and thousands of sparks were sent out in a giant puff.

Most of the girls were elated, believing that with nowhere else to house them, the administration would have no choice but to free them. They believed they had won the night. However, it would be a short-lived victory.

As the flames slowly died on the ruins of Chamberlain Hall, Agnes MacNaughton spoke sharply to Estelle Stott, her secretary and right-hand woman, her disciplinarian, and sometimes her substitute. She ordered that every girl staying in Chamberlain be brought to the reception room of Tufts. Then she marched off, leaving the silent teachers and still-giddy girls watching her stiff figure fade into the darkness.

Thirty girls, all beginning to shiver in the quickly chilling March night, were shepherded into Tufts in their nightgowns. They were left alone while Miss MacNaughton met with Miss Stott, Miss Crenshaw, Miss Ross, and Miss Markham. Josephine French whispered to Margaret Abernethy, wondering if this would be the last time they would have to wait outside Miss MacNaughton's office to learn their fates. It was certainly not the first time for either of them.

In her office Miss MacNaughton turned on the teachers with a fierce intensity. She told them that they must get confessions from those who were guilty and that they must get the most dangerous ones off the grounds immediately to prevent more fires. She turned to her most trusted employee, Miss Stott, and ordered her to do the questioning, with the rest of the women serving as witnesses to the interrogation.

The women returned to the reception room where the girls stood waiting and talking conspiratorially among themselves. They hushed at once when the women entered, and all eyes went first to Miss MacNaughton, who would not meet their gazes, and then to Miss Stott, whose glare told them exactly who was in control at that moment. The girls were disappointed that Miss MacNaughton was not taking charge. Miss Stott was known to be more brutal and less compassionate than any of the other women. Several of the girls even began to question the strategy they had manufactured in hopes of getting sent home.

Miss Stott began in a voice that did not need volume or tone to make an impression. Her words alone imparted both rage and authority. She told the girls that those who had not had anything to do with the fires should go with Miss Crenshaw and the other matrons. Those who knew about the fires or had anything to do with starting them must confess. Then she demanded that the guilty ones move into the teachers' reception room, and she pointed to the double wooden doors leading to the room where teachers not on duty ate their meals.

Thirty girls followed her arm with their eyes, but only sixteen girls shuffled through those doors. Taking confidence from their sheer number, some of them held hands in solidarity. The rest of the girls, relieved to have their participation so easily dismissed, left with Miss Crenshaw but kept their gaze on the sixteen as the wooden doors closed tightly. What would await these girls who had so easily been convinced to confess?

The only ones who knew for a fact what went on in that room were the ones behind those doors, but one thing was certain: different stories emerged from that meeting and someone, maybe many, later lied about what happened. What questions were asked, what answers were given, and who confessed could never be agreed on, even though there were many witnesses.

By the time the sheriff arrived later that night, those sixteen had been divided into two groups. Six girls—Josephine French, Bertha Hall, Wilma Owens, Margaret Pridgen, Dolores Seawell, and Pearl Stiles—were led away, still in their nightgowns, by the sheriff and taken to the Moore County Jail in Carthage, where they slept in one cell, sharing the two cots that awaited them. The next day after more questioning by Miss Stott, the other ten—Margaret Abernethy, Mary Lee Bronson, Edna Clark, Thelma Council, Ollie Harding, Virginia Hayes, Marian Mercer, Rosa Mull, Chloe Stillwell, and Estelle Wilson—would join them and fill up the other three cells in the jailhouse. They would become known as the Samarcand Sixteen.

Part One

THE SAMARCAND SIXTEEN

ONE

To comprehend fully why the Samarcand Sixteen ended up at the school and why they would risk their lives and reputations to get out, it is necessary to consider the social environment of North Carolina in the 1930s. The girls were living out patterns established by people they could not imagine and were tied by cultural restraints that had been put on them long before they were born.

North Carolina was in the powerful throes of a eugenics movement. Eugenics was based on the belief that the quality of a society could be improved by encouraging the strong, intelligent, and economically and genetically superior members of that society to produce more children and by discouraging the poor, ignorant, and physically weak members from reproducing. The Samarcand Sixteen fell squarely in this second category. They were generally poor white girls who held the potential for breeding more poor white children—or worse, mixed-race children; North Carolina, along with much of the rest of the world, was determined to keep that from happening.

Many proponents considered eugenics to be a science rather than a social philosophy. It was held in high regard during the first decades of the twentieth century, supported by such prominent figures as Winston Churchill, Alexander Graham Bell, Margaret Sanger, Theodore Roosevelt, H. G. Wells, George Bernard Shaw, and H. L. Mencken, who once suggested that the U.S. government pay one thousand dollars each to all Americans deemed "undesirable" if they would be voluntarily sterilized.

Earnest Hooten, a physical anthropologist known for his racist and classist writings, likened eugenics to Noah's Ark, in which in order to survive and thrive, some of the more "noxious creatures" must be left behind (398). The theory became popular, especially with people who believed themselves to be in the superior class. In a 1939 article, Julian L. Woodward, a leader in the field of public opinion research, delineated the goals of eugenics to be first "protecting man's position in nature" by cultivating the traits that proved his "pre-cultural evolutionary value," and second, breeding "a race that can attain a higher plane of living" (471). Others have defined it a bit more simply: for example, Gerald V. O'Brien stated that "eugenics policies can include any measures designed to ensure that the 'best' members of a society reproduce in greater numbers, or that the reproductive opportunities of the 'worst' members are limited, either voluntarily or, more often, by force" (3).

The origins of eugenics can be traced to almost seventy years before the girls at Samarcand decided to burn down two buildings, and the inspiration for it came from quite a notable source. In 1859, in his *On the Origin of Species,* Charles Darwin posited that all creatures evolve in accordance with their heredity and environment. Darwin's cousin Francis Galton was inspired by Darwin's theories and began developing his own perspective on the ideas. Galton had traveled widely as a young man, gaining knowledge and acquiring prejudices. In the 1860s he returned to London with a firm belief in the hierarchy of human beings, with Anglo-Saxons securely established at the top. He began thinking about the state of humanity and how to improve it, and he theorized that people could be bred, like dogs and racehorses, to create better human beings and therefore a superior society. "What Nature does blindly, slowly, and ruthlessly, man may do providently, quickly, and kindly," he wrote in his *Essays on Eugenics* (Galton 24–25). By encouraging the right people to procreate and discouraging the wrong people from reproducing, humans could intervene in the process of evolution. He called his theory "eugenics," from the Greek meaning "well born." In fact Galton did not invent anything new but simply gave a name to popular theories of his day.

Galton focused much of his writing on positive eugenics—that is, the encouragement of the best and brightest people to reproduce more often. In the words of Ava Chamberlain, Galton gathered

> hundreds of genealogies of judges, politicians, authors, musicians, scientists, clergymen, and turning his attention from "brain" to "muscle," oarsmen and wrestlers. Analysis of this data led him to the two-part position that would define the eugenics movement throughout its history. From the observation that human ability "clings to certain families," he concluded that intellect, talent, and even moral character were hereditary traits. This theoretical claim had an important practical application. "It would be quite practicable," he asserted, "to produce a highly-gifted race of men by judicious marriages during several consecutive generations." Just as horses could be bred to win races, the

> results of human reproduction were "largely, though indirectly, under our control." (168–69)

It was not long, however, before the idea of negative eugenics—the discouragement of the poorest of the population pool to procreate—became more popular. The poor and ignorant were holding back progress and consuming resources at an increasing rate because hygiene, medicine, and social policies were helping them to endure and therefore reproduce. These factors had, in fact, become "rather dangerous enemies of human progress," according to advocates of eugenics (Kuhl 13). Therefore the emphasis was put on stemming the tide of a growing population that was unwanted; as O'Brien described it, "eugenics interests were primarily stoked by dystopian rather than utopian considerations" (4).

Around the turn of the twentieth century, the experiments done by the Austrian scientist Gregor Johann Mendel in the 1850s and 1860s were rediscovered by eugenicists. Mendel had worked with pea plants and identified the role of dominant and recessive genes. He concluded that the plants were much more influenced by genes than by environment, and this fact inspired eugenicists in their quest for a better society. Because Mendel's findings were that environment determined little, eugenicists came to discount the role of education and social programs in helping the underprivileged. The only way, it appeared, to improve the human race was by keeping inferior types from reproducing.

Support for this theory came from Richard L. Dugdale, who in 1874 became interested in "the genealogy of degeneracy" (Larson 19) after taking part in an inspection of conditions at a jail in upstate New York as part of a prison reform movement. While there, he discovered that six of the criminals he interviewed were related. He began to investigate the family—to whom he assigned the name "Jukes"—in an attempt to understand the origins of crime and criminals. He traced the family five generations back to six sisters. After interviewing 709 related people, he determined that over half were criminals, prostitutes, or relief recipients who had cost the public more than $2 million in the courts, in the prisons, and in relief aid.

Dugdale did not discount the role of environment in the development of families such as the Jukeses. He made a statement that undercut the tenets of eugenics: "Environment tends to produce habits which may become hereditary especially so in pauperism and licentiousness" (Dugdale 57). He further explained, "The tendency of heredity is to produce an environment which perpetuates that heredity: thus, the licentious parent makes an example which greatly aids in fixing habits of debauchery in the child" (Dugdale 65). The only way to "break a chain of hereditary degeneracy in humans," then, "was to remove the children of social misfits from their families and give them vocational training in a healthy environment" (Larson 20).

A later analysis in 1915, however, changed the focus to mental acuity and increased the number studied to over twenty-eight hundred. This study categorized participants not by their "sins"—that is, poverty or licentiousness—but by mental ability. The analysis claimed that over half of those studied were feebleminded. As Larson explained, "This finding was crucial for eugenicists because they viewed 'feeblemindedness,' which included various levels of mental retardation, as an inherited unit characteristic" (21). Inherited feeblemindedness discounted, then, the role of the environment because no environmental change for the better could improve a feebleminded brain. The only solution, therefore, for families such as the Jukeses—a burden on society in numerous ways—was segregation and sterilization for each and every one of them.

The study concluded that idiots begat idiots and criminals begat criminals. In subsequent years many problems with the studies were discovered, but at the time it appeared that eugenicists were right: the poor and feebleminded were reproducing much faster than the well-to-do and educated were, and society was suffering because of this. The American Eugenics Society in the 1920s proved that sterilizing the initial Jukeses would have cost $150. The white race, eugenicists believed, could have been immensely improved for such a small cost, and society must keep such a tragedy from happening again.

In 1925 Clarence Darrow published an essay in the *American Mercury* disputing the results of the Jukes study and those of its polar opposite, a study of the family who came from the early New England theologian and evangelist Jonathan Edwards. Proponents of positive eugenics had long maintained that "greatness" had come from Edwards's line, including "12 college presidents, 265 college graduates, 65 college professors, 60 physicians, 100 clergymen, 75 army officers, 60 prominent authors, 100 lawyers, 30 judges, 80 public officers, 3 governors, mayors, and State officials, 3 congressmen, 2 United States senators, and 1 Vice President" (Darrow 152). The problem with assigning greatness to the Edwards line and depravity to that of the Jukes family was an "elementary error in logic: 'after this, because of this,'" and that if someone went looking for either greatness or depravity, he would probably find it. On the question of feeblemindedness in the Jukes family, Darrow argued, "But what is feeble-mindedness, anyway? I submit that it is entirely out of the question to find out whether a person is feeble-minded fifty or a hundred years after his death. The only way that feeble-mindedness can even be approximately determined is by a thorough and elaborate mental test, which could not possibly have been given in these cases" (Darrow 156).

Darrow compared the Edwards and Jukes families and determined that "some men may preach hell-fire sermons, or make speeches in the Senate and the court room. Others do the rough work of the world. Which are the most important in the scheme of life, assuming that there is any scheme of life?" If he were forced to choose either Max Jukes or Jonathan Edwards for a neighbor, he concluded, "I am free to confess that I would take Max without a moment's hesitation" (157).

Despite arguments such as Darrow's, however, the belief in eugenics, both positive and negative, persisted. In 1910 Charles Benedict Davenport, a biologist from Harvard, "transformed Galton's theory into an American crusade" (Chamberlain 173). He opened the Eugenics Record Office in Cold Springs Harbor on Long Island and sent out eugenics field workers to "compile pedigrees of 'feeble-minded' families" to support the theories. The studies sometimes had visual aids: "Some included photographs that illustrated the 'unmistakable look of the feeble-minded'" (Chamberlain 170).

By the 1920s these prevailing ideas about genetics and the worth—or lack of worth—of certain types of persons were embedded deeply in society. In *The Fruit of the Family Tree,* a best seller published in 1926, Albert Wiggam wrote frankly:

> Finally, then, we see, actually and literally, that from dogs to kings, from rats to college presidents, blood always tells. The one central problem of progress, the endless task of statesmanship and education, is, therefore, to bring about those economic conditions, these social, political, and educational ideals and opportunities which encourage those of good blood to mate with their own kind and produce good families of children, at least more than are produced by stocks of mediocre blood; and to institute stern measures which will insure that those of positively bad blood produce no children at all. Such a race of people can easily run on through vicissitudes of time, creating ideals, building institutions of worth and grandeur, and developing a culture, all of which are simply the outward expressions of the ceaseless energy of noble blood. Such a people and only such can build great civilizations—civilizations that will continue amid happiness and achievement. (20–21)

But how could such a grand idea of improvement of the race be accomplished? Who gets to decide who is superior? What standards are used to determine who is allowed to reproduce? How does a society get one part of its population to reduce its number?

Alfred Ploetz, a German race hygienist, offered one rather drastic solution during World War I when he suggested that "the mentally and physically weak" should be put on the front lines as "cannon fodder" (Kuhl 31). While shocking, this suggests how poorly regarded and easily dismissed the underprivileged and mentally challenged were during these years. This is hardly the only time in history that such thinking occurred. Similar dehumanization of a marginalized group was seen in the treatment of Native Americans and African slaves. In addition, of course, it could be seen to an extreme degree in the 1930s and 1940s in Germany's treatment of the Jews.

The search for a eugenics solution continued by other means. The first step was to identify the "undesirable" persons. In 1908 this was made easier by the new IQ tests that were brought to the United States from France by the American psychologist and eugenicist H. H. Goddard. The Benet-Simon test—later called simply the IQ test—became a way to quantify mental ability and identify people who, according to eugenicists, should not reproduce. Goddard identified three levels of disability: "high-grade morons"; "middle-grade imbeciles"; and "low-grade idiots," terms that became commonplace in society, along with the more commonly used description "feebleminded." These terms became useful with eugenicists as they searched for a way to keep the undesirables from reproducing. In fact, during the first decade of the twentieth century, feeblemindedness became the focus of eugenicists, and "eugenic unfitness came to be inextricably connected to moronity" (O'Brien 164).

Once inferior persons were identified, the question became how to keep such people from procreating. Larson listed four different methods for restricting the birth of children: "marriage laws, sexual segregation, involuntary sterilization, and limits on immigration" (22). Many states, including North Carolina, passed laws in the 1910s restricting the right to marry between the physically deformed, the ill, or the feebleminded, but eugenicists quickly realized that the act of prohibiting marriage would not keep people from reproducing.

Segregation of those deemed unfit became too cost prohibitive. There were simply not enough facilities to house all who needed them. Nearly all states attempted to segregate some people, however: the mentally ill, the feebleminded, and the criminal. Asylums, prisons, and training schools popped up all over the country in an attempt to restrict the sexuality of individuals as well as to give help to those in need.

With marriage laws and segregation working less than effectively and immigration restriction solving only part of the population problem, sterilization—either voluntary or forced—became the favored weapon of eugenicists. In the first two decades of the twentieth century many individual states passed sterilization laws, but when challenged in court, these were often overturned for violating human rights. Some states were more successful, however. California, for example, forcibly sterilized thousands of its citizens, resulting in more than 80 percent of national sterilizations by 1921; ultimately the state sterilized twenty thousand people before the law was repealed in the 1960s. Sterilization was "touted as a public health measure" in many places, "as if feeblemindedness were a virus that could be transmitted between people" (O'Brien 40). The Supreme Court even compared it to compulsory vaccinations.

Despite challenges to sterilization laws, the Supreme Court eventually upheld a state's right to force sterilization in 1927's *Buck vs. Bell.* Carrie Buck was born to her mother, Emma, in 1906. She had a younger sister, Doris, and a brother, Roy. Soon after the birth of her third child, Emma was committed to the Virginia State Colony for Epileptics and Feebleminded because, the state said, she was immoral and had syphilis. Carrie was adopted by John and Alice Dobbs and attended school until the sixth grade. At age seventeen she became pregnant and was committed to the same institution where her mother was held, sent there by her adoptive parents, who claimed they could not take care of her and that she had become "incorrigible." The superintendent of the institution, Dr. Albert Sidney Priddy, filed a petition with the board of directors to forcibly sterilize Carrie because her mother had been tested and found to have a mental age of eight, and it was believed that Carrie was at risk for the same kind of immoral life her mother had presumably led—evidenced by the fact that Carrie had already become pregnant out of wedlock. In truth, it was discovered later that Carrie had been raped by her adoptive mother's nephew and that the family had sent her to the institution to save their family's reputation. Carrie's illegitimate daughter, Vivian, was born and raised for a time by the Dobbses. She too was determined to be feebleminded—even though she later attended school in Virginia and was listed on the honor roll in 1931 before she died from complications from measles in 1932.

Carrie did not want to be sterilized. She got a lawyer, and the case ended up in the Supreme Court, which ruled against Carrie 8–1. She received a form of tubal ligation. The court accepted that Carrie was promiscuous without any evidence and said that the sterilization did not deny her any rights since she was housed in a state institution—and anyway, the sterilization was not designed to be punitive, only helpful to Carrie in living a better life. In the ruling Justice Oliver Wendell Holmes famously concluded that "three generations of imbeciles are enough." "It is better for all the world," he argued, "if instead of waiting to execute degenerate offspring for crime, or to let them starve for their imbecility, society can prevent those who are manifestly unfit from continuing their kind." Carrie's sister, Doris, was sterilized later during an appendectomy—without her knowledge or consent—to make sure the family would not reproduce. Doris, who later tried to have children, did not discover what had been done to her until 1980. Carrie lived out her life as a domestic worker in Virginia and died in 1983 in a nursing home. Those who studied and interviewed her in her later years seemed to agree that she was of normal intelligence. This ruling increased the number of sterilizations in the United States in the 1930s by 1,000 percent, making it the decade with more legal eugenic sterilizations than any other decade in American history (Currell and Cogdell 2).

While the eugenics movement was international—spawning several global conferences and university majors—it was especially popular in the American South. The South was no stranger to the idea of controlling and intervening in reproduction: many slave owners had attempted to create a better breed of slave by forcing sex between specific partners. In addition the South was struggling with its cultural identity in the twentieth century. The cult of the "Lost Cause" left over from the Civil War still haunted the South and led many to see the area as beyond cultural resuscitation. In 1920 H. L. Mencken had written his scathing attack "The Sahara of the Bozart," in which he claimed that the region had been "drained of all its best blood" by the Civil War—in other words, the aristocratic blood had been reduced, diluted, and polluted, leaving "the land to the harsh mercies of the poor white trash, now its masters." Could the South possibly stem the tide of poverty and illiteracy that plagued its boundaries, or would the poor and illiterate simply take over through sheer force of numbers? The fear of this actually happening made the South a haven for eugenic thought.

As cities and towns began to grow in the South, filled with workers from rural areas, some saw prosperity in the transformation, but others saw problems instead: "unruliness, illicit sexuality, and high rates of out-of-wedlock pregnancy and venereal disease" (Cahn 49). As young rural girls of the working class moved to towns and cities to find work after World War

I, along the way exploring new forms of entertainment such as dancing, joyriding, and attending movies, the problems only seemed to increase. The new sexual mores of the 1920s were disturbing and alarming to many people, who simply did not know what to do with adolescents—especially girls who had taken it upon themselves to exercise their freedom. Many believed that the "adolescent's body had surged ahead of the mind's capacity for reason and emotional control" and that therefore the teenage years were rife with danger for teens as well as those affected by their behavior (Cahn 21). The legal age for a young woman to have consensual sex was only fourteen in North Carolina, "adding to the belief that these girls were 'deliberate actors'" participating in immoral conduct (Cahn 45). With all this in mind, these young women became the population on which eugenicists focused as they attempted to control the quality of the white race.

While this migration of country to city was repeated throughout the United States, it was considered especially dangerous in the South, where the image of the white woman on a pedestal, graciously and demurely attending to men, was still very much alive. This new youth-crazed modern society came directly into conflict with the Victorian models still found in the South. Diverse groups such as fundamentalist preachers, educators, and the Ku Klux Klan all campaigned against the modern youth culture that included young women exploring their world without proper chaperones or even a code of ethics. They agreed "that the younger generation—especially bold daughters—posed a threat to the moral fabric of southern society" (Cahn 27). In a 1922 sermon at Charlotte's Calvary Methodist Church, Rev. J. A. Sharp went so far as to say that young women "park their corsets on the outside of the pavilion and throw decency to the wind, exclaiming, 'Come on, boys, the sky is the limit.'"

The problem of white women and sex was not a new one, as Susan K. Cahn has explained. The South was well aware of the consequences of sexual freedom for white women:

"Accusations of 'unruly' or 'disorderly' female sexuality reached back to the antebellum period, a time when the extra-marital or interracial involvements of poor white women were perceived as especially threatening to a social order that depended on white women's sexual purity for the orderly transmission of property and racial identity" (Cahn 54). In fact it became easier simply to label sexually active poor white girls as feebleminded because of their desires and their inadequate educations. They became "females who were classified as morons or as otherwise hereditarily defective" and "were generally identified as sexually immoral and incapable of controlling their

Samarcand Manor building.
Courtesy of the State Archives of North Carolina.

base desires" (O'Brien 143). Such a woman became the most common southern sterilization victim in the 1930s and 1940s: "a single, sexually active, working-class white teenage girl with one or no children and a low IQ score" (Cahn 160). These women "exposed the southern myth of virtuous white womanhood, toppling a longstanding [*sic*] pillar in the defense of white privilege and racial segregation" (Cahn 160).

Segregation followed by sterilization became the chief goal of eugenicists for these poor white teens. As a result, "training schools" were created for young white men and women in the second decade of the twentieth century; these were institutions where sexes were segregated and sterilizations could be performed as part of regular health care. By 1924 fifty-seven publicly funded institutions for delinquent girls existed in the United States. Only two states failed to establish such an institution (Cahn 46). One of these schools, in the sand hills of North Carolina, was Samarcand Manor Training School for Delinquent Girls, established by the North Carolina legislature in 1917 to give "troubled" girls a chance to mend their ways and change their lives for the better. At least that was the publicized goal.

If a young woman was suspected of "running around with boys," she could be sent to Samarcand by local law enforcement for rehabilitation. Other girls, though, were sent to Samarcand by their parents, many of whom claimed they just did not know what to do with their misbehaving daughters and so wanted the state of North Carolina to take them off their hands. Still other girls ended up at the training school because of extreme circumstances in their families that had nothing to do with misbehavior. For example, orphaned girls were occasionally sent there because North Carolinians did not know what to do with them: either the orphanages were full or the girls were considered too old. Some who were victims of incest were sent to Samarcand as a protection against further abuse.

In other words, while Samarcand was started with the idea of giving girls a second chance in life, it eventually became a dumping ground for girls with problems that their families and the government could not fix any other way. Many of their problems were sexual in nature. When it opened, Samarcand was partially funded by federal money earmarked for the prevention of sexually transmitted diseases, tying the girls' misbehavior expressly to sexuality.

The *Public Welfare Progress* newsletter, published by the North Carolina State Board of Charities and Public Welfare, reported one example in 1926 of a school superintendent in a small county who said, "Two girls in this county are beyond control and the only way we can handle them is to put them in jail. They are very immoral, and are doing much damage to the community where they live" (7.11). The superintendent overlooked the fact that such immorality required a male participant as well; males generally went without punishment. These two girls ended up at Samarcand simply because they could not stay in jail and the sheriff did not want to release them.

In many ways the intent of such schools sounded honorable. A member of the State Board of Charities and Public Welfare, Kate Ford Peele, wrote in an op-ed piece for the *Elizabeth City Daily Advance* that Samarcand "was established not to punish girls but to help them, to redeem them from wrong living and bad environments while they are young and impressionable. Such an institution, it was believed, would help to reduce the criminal class and add to the State's quota of good citizens" (April 22, 1931). The *Public Welfare Progress* in 1923 touted it as a model for institutions of its kind in the country and described the inmates as "clean, bright-looking, healthy girls . . . who closely resemble the student body of the usual boarding-school," although the article admitted that most were "sex offenders" and the rest were "unruly or wayward" (4.7).

The male equivalent of Samarcand existed, but boys were sent there exclusively for breaking the law and rarely for sexual indiscretions. Boys were given much more leeway about exploring their sexuality with a variety of partners—especially if the girls involved were poor or black—and their behavior was tolerated, even celebrated, by society. In fact scientists believed that "whereas men were rational self-possessed sexual actors, women were driven by irrational passions unknowable at the conscious level—particularly during adolescence" (Cahn 59). Therefore girls who committed the same acts as boys seemed in the eyes of southern traditionalists to be rejecting irrationally all that the South deemed honorable. Many of the young men were sterilized, though, as the eugenics movement hit a high pitch, in order to reduce the criminal population. Castration was the early choice of doctors, and the goal became sterilizing every boy before he was released. Eventually doctors performed vasectomies instead.

Prejudice against teens regarding their sexuality weighed heaviest, though, on poor white girls. Class, race, and gender all worked against the Samarcand inmates. Girls of the higher classes were kept in check mainly through private clubs, schools, and elite social events. They were simply sent away to boarding school or married off quickly if they became unruly, promiscuous, or disobedient. Black girls were under less scrutiny because most white people considered sexuality and rebellion part of their genetic makeup—they could not help it, the logic went—and this misconception about black girls' sexuality kept them out of training schools, at least in the 1920s and 1930s. But what could be done with poor white girls who chose to have indiscriminate sex? The solution became to lock them up, usually for an indefinite time or until they became old enough that the state and their parents had no legal control over them. Along with confinement to keep these girls from becoming mothers to children who would repeat their bad behavior, many of the girls were sterilized. In fact eventually over three hundred sterilizations would be done at Samarcand, including perhaps on some of the Samarcand Sixteen.

At any one time the school might house 250 girls, although at the time of the 1931 fires, it was overcrowded with around 275. Girls as young as six and as old as twenty were sent there either by their families or by the law, usually for being drunkards or prostitutes, or simply for being in danger of becoming such women. Sometimes the charge was as simple as running away from home. The girls were considered "fallen," a word used as an all-encompassing adjective to describe any behavior considered bad enough to threaten society. Once in trouble, girls were stigmatized forever, considered tainted, damaged goods and therefore in need of incarceration and rehabilitation or at least removal from society.

The school and dormitories of Samarcand were built on a former estate that had been left to the state of North Carolina when the owner died. It was named after a city in central Asia known for its ancient crafts. The land sloped gently down from the white-pillared main house—used as the

Samarcand girls outside the chapel. Courtesy of the State Archives of North Carolina.

administration building—to a picturesque lake surrounded by pine trees, redbuds, and dogwoods. Open spaces, playgrounds, and gardens were scattered around the buildings, and there girls could be found working, studying, or lounging. The sand hills of Moore County were known as the hottest part of North Carolina, but the tall trees offered abundant shade, and often a cool breeze would blow through. The buildings and grounds were reminders of a gracious Old South, but just as with that antebellum world, Samarcand was not exactly what it appeared to be.

The first superintendent was Agnes MacNaughton, a woman whom the secretary of the Samarcand board, Mrs. J. R. Chamberlain, described as maintaining "thorough control" over the girls at the school. This was an understatement: MacNaughton was a stern, stiff woman with dark eyes and a thin tight line where her lips met; her wavy hair was pulled back into a tight bun to control the curl. MacNaughton considered one of the main problems of the girls sent to Samarcand to be a lack of self-control that resulted in bad behavior that was both genetic and habitual. These girls came from negative family environments, she believed, and had not been disciplined enough at home. She saw it as her role to enforce that discipline while they were under her charge—a tactic that included all forms of punishment both physical and psychological. She was not alone in her pessimistic opinion of the girls. In a master's thesis called "Case Studies of Delinquent Girls in North Carolina," written in 1927 at the University of North Carolina, Margaret C. Brietz, a clear believer in eugenics, concluded that the girls she interviewed were depraved simply because of heredity.

Much of what went on at the school was hidden from public knowledge as a necessary way, MacNaughton thought, of securing control. The public image was that Samarcand was clean and well organized. According to the official reports, food was abundant, the cooking was excellent, and girls spent their days learning basic academic skills; studying the Bible, manners, and music; playing sports; and performing domestic skills such as milking, feeding of animals, weaving, canning, doing laundry, and gardening. It was only when girls did not appreciate their opportunities or obey the strict but arbitrary rules that they were sent to the discipline hall and given extra work. By 1931, though, this version of life at Samarcand was just a fairy tale.

On the night of March 12, a group of girls decided they simply could not tolerate the conditions any longer and that they would rather be anywhere else than in an institution where they were subjected to whippings, being locked in their rooms, and sleepless nights battling the roaches and bedbugs. They were in Samarcand because they were poor white females and because they had been, generally, sexually active. Advocates of eugenics had sentenced these girls to incarceration and a restriction of their individual rights because of the "sins" of class, race, and gender—conditions over which they had no control.

Rumor had it that the school sometimes released girls who refused to reform and were therefore considered incorrigible and beyond rehabilitation. Good behavior had gotten these girls nowhere, so what did they have to lose? Some of them believed that extreme misbehavior was a ticket home, and they were willing to risk everything for that one chance. According to Susan Cahn, in her study of sexuality and the southern girl, "From institutional records, it is clear that the quickest route out of Samarcand was not reform but defiance. Staff frequently judged the most difficult inmates as beyond rehabilitation and promptly returned them to their home communities" (64–65). The girls were counting on just this.

TWO

After the sixteen girls were taken to the Carthage jail, a hearing was held on March 16, during which Judge George R. Humber appointed George W. McNeill as defense attorney with Don Phillips, solicitor of the Thirteenth District, as prosecutor. None of the girls had a personal lawyer, most likely because all of them were poor and relatively uneducated, and their families were in counties far away from Carthage without the means to come to their daughters' defense either physically or financially. In essence, the girls were on their own, and each had to rely on the services of an attorney who was also defending fifteen other girls—and who was not really invested in the trial's outcome. He was doing a job he had been forced to take rather than taking on a fight he believed in at his core.

Without a good and involved lawyer to advise them what to say in court, the girls naively confessed to the judge that they had taken part in the fires. On March 18 the *News and Observer* (Raleigh) summed up what the girls said in the hearing:

> Margaret Pridgen admitted she was present the second time Chamberlain Hall was set on fire and let it burn.
>
> Wilma Owens testified that she knew all about the burning of the two buildings, where the fire was started and when they were started.
>
> Virginia Hayes testified that she started the fire in her room also in a back room, [and] Rosa Mull said she helped to start the fires.
>
> Edna Clark testified she started a fire in her room and that Marion [*sic*] Mercer, Ollie Harding and Margaret Abernethy assisted her in starting the fires. Estelle Wilson and Chloe Stilwell [*sic*] admitted setting fire to the curtains in the living room.
>
> Josephine French admitted that she helped burn Chamberlain Hall.

The jail was vastly overcrowded in Carthage, so a few days after the hearing, nine of the girls were sent by school bus almost eighty miles away to the

Robeson County Jail in Lumberton so that all the defendants could be held more comfortably. Once arriving in Lumberton, the girls became minor celebrities, giving interviews and receiving gifts of cigarettes, magazines, and hair ribbons.

The *News and Observer* reported on March 24 that Margaret Pridgen, from Carthage, was especially taken with her newfound celebrity status, and she spoke freely and openly to the press about her involvement in the fires. In fact one article reported that she took complete responsibility for organizing and starting the fires. She claimed she was tired of Samarcand and believed that by burning the buildings she would be moved to another, better place or sent home. "I'd do it again," she boasted, adding, "Sometimes I just feel mean."

The press made a great deal about the fact that the girls were taken to jail in their nightgowns and therefore lacked proper clothing. The same article intimated that the lack of clothing indicated loose morals on the girls' part: "The girls are almost minus clothing, but the modesty of most of them seems not affected. As the Pridgen girl, scantily clad, told of her part in the affair, a cigarette rolled out on the floor from the bed on which she was sitting. About her other girls listened or took part in the conversation, some wearing only raincoats or a couple of pieces of clothing." Their lawyer, McNeill, did not seem to be giving them any advice about what to say to the press. Public opinion did not mean much to him, and the girls dug themselves deeper and deeper into guilt in the eyes of the people. But that was about to change.

Miles away from the Robeson County Jail, on March 26, Nell Battle Lewis sat on her back porch in the pale spring sunlight awaiting the morning mail. Lewis was not a typical southern woman of her times who concerned herself with society and gossip. Instead she was a progressive woman whose influential column in the *News and Observer,* "Incidentally," covered politics, public welfare, and women's rights.

She lived alone in her newly built house across the street from one of the best schools for girls in the South—and her alma mater—St. Mary's. Lewis had been a crusader for women's rights and labor rights for more than a decade, and just twelve days earlier she had received her license to practice law, a move she hoped would help her in her pursuit of justice for those whose voices were least heard in society.

When the mail arrived, she found one letter that especially piqued her interest. It was from Mrs. Thomas E. Williams of Leaksville, North Carolina, a woman Lewis knew slightly from her work in the women's rights movement. She opened the envelope and began to read the short letter. It concerned

Nell Battle Lewis home, 1514 St. Mary's, Raleigh. Photograph by the author.

Virginia Hayes, who had been charged with first-degree arson for burning down the two buildings at Samarcand Manor. Virginia had been a resident of Leaksville before being sent to Samarcand for running away from home, Mrs. Williams mentioned, and the town's citizens felt they had a stake in the case. Lewis was intrigued and read the brief letter several times, especially the three paragraphs that asked for her help:

> I cannot feel that this child and her unfortunate companions are the hardened criminals that this charge would indicate, and believe that they should have legal counsel, who will give their case a more thorough investigation and a deeper interest than it could receive from attorneys appointed by the court.
>
> This is to enquire if your services can be secured to represent these parties, especially the Hayes child, and in case you can handle the matter, I will thank you to take charge of the defense.
>
> My only interest in the matter is that the idea of these children's being tried for a capital crime is so revolting to my sense of justice that I feel impelled to aid in securing competent counsel for them.

Lewis was delighted with the prospect. This was exactly the kind of case she had hoped to take on when she received her law degree: helping those with less of a voice in society find justice. She immediately began to organize her thoughts and make plans, doing research on the case as well as the crime of first-degree arson. A month later, on April 24, she set out for Carthage to meet with Virginia and the other six defendants there. While there, she tried to call on George McNeill, who lived in Carthage, but was unable to find him at his office, so she slipped her card under the door. Later that night she wrote him a letter:

> I am very sorry that I was not able to locate you when I was in Carthage today. No doubt you got my card which I left under your office door.
>
> Certain ladies in Leaksville who are interested in Virginia Hayes, one of the girls held in connection with the burnings at Samarcand, have employed me to represent this girl in the coming trial. I was in Carthage today to talk with her and the other six defendants now in jail there, and as you have already been connected with their case I wished, of course, to have a conference with you about the matter. I shall probably be in Carthage again before long, and I trust that then I shall have the pleasure of seeing you.
>
> I am sure that you agree with me in feeling that these unfortunate girls should have their case presented as effectively as possible, and I hope that you will give me the benefit of your ability and experience to that end, and that I shall have the honor of being associated with you in their defense.

Carthage was the county seat of Moore County where Samarcand was located. It was a terribly poor county with the exception of the two resort communities of Southern Pines and Pinehurst, which were islands of wealth. The contrast between the two resort towns and the rest of the county illustrated sharply the poverty that most of the population was experiencing. The land that is now Pinehurst was originally 6,000 acres of pine forest, which was cut for lumber, leaving a barren, sandy stretch of useless property, like most of the rest of the county. James Walker Tufts, a Boston philanthropist, purchased the land for about one dollar an acre in the late 1890s in hopes of creating a health resort for the middle class, although many people called this folly. With such activities as riding, hunting, polo, lawn bowling, bicycling, and archery, however, it was destined to become a playground for the rich. A few years later Tufts added golf, which led the area to become one of the premier golf resorts in the United States. Southern Pines too was designed to be a health resort. John T. Patrick bought 674 acres—for about twice as much an acre as Tufts paid—in the 1880s with the idea of creating a community where the dry air could cure the ailments of visitors. Although it never became what he envisioned, it did become one of the favorite winter getaway resorts for northerners. It also became a gathering place for the arts, and prominent writers such as Thomas Wolfe, F. Scott Fitzgerald, and Paul Green took up temporary residence there.

In the rest of Moore County, however, most people were suffering intensely from the Great Depression, although it had never been a prosperous place to live even before the 1930s. The sandy soil made agricultural work difficult, and there was little other work to be done. This trial, it occurred to Lewis, would put this tiny county on the map, and she planned on helping it do just that.

What Lewis did not know yet when she wrote McNeill was that he would be happy to take Lewis on as a colleague, and in fact she would end up shouldering the majority of the research, the preparation, and the trial itself. McNeill wrote back to her on the 27th, apologized for being absent—he said he was in Pinehurst—and replied that he would be glad *to assist her* in defending the girls rather than the other way around—a move that would allow him more time to pursue his real interest: managing real estate in Moore County and perhaps playing more golf in Pinehurst. He had been appointed to this case, and in his experience he had never known a controversial trial to do much for his image or career. Passing it off to an inexperienced female lawyer seemed like the answer to a prayer, a gift he would not pass up. Whether Lewis took the lead or he did, he would still be paid twenty-five dollars per girl at the end of the trial.

Later the two lawyers would add the services of Claude Woltz to assist them in research. Woltz, who had recently moved to Carthage because he married a local girl, was a World War I veteran who had served as a judge advocate in France. Besides studying law, he was interested in researching the legal implications of social conditions and psychology. He would turn out to be much more help to Lewis than McNeill because of her eventual defense strategy, and she would come to count on his advice where psychology and sociology were involved.

Cornelia Battle Lewis, called Nell, grew up in an ultra-conservative family who believed firmly in a society divided by race, class, and gender. Her father did not approve of college for women—even going so far as to support a limit on the dormitory space allotted to women at the University of North Carolina at Chapel Hill—but he relented under pressure from his only daughter and allowed her to attend Goucher College in Baltimore for a year and then Smith College in Massachusetts to finish her degree.

Nell Lewis had long resented the gender limits put on her by her family and resisted the strictness of the rules of a culture that expected her to fulfill the ideal of southern womanhood. In the North she blossomed, and she returned home with her head filled with liberal ideas that chafed against the beliefs held by her father, stepmother, and three half brothers, the youngest of whom was almost a decade older than Nell. When her brothers realized the influence the North had on cementing her progressive ideas, they were appalled to the extent that they limited their own daughters' educations to the conservative and decidedly southern college Sweet Briar, in Virginia. They were not going to take any chances that another feminist might emerge in the family.

After college Lewis went to France during World War I, where she participated in the canteen service with the American Expeditionary Force from 1918 to 1919, and her time in Europe only expanded her liberal views. It was there that she entered into a romance with a young officer, Lenoir Chambers, who would later win a Pulitzer Prize for his writings about racial equality. When she came home, though, and introduced Chambers to her father, the relationship began to fizzle, mainly due to her father's influence. Her father believed that his daughter had inherited her mother's mental instability, and so he was always on the lookout for proof of a breakdown in her. He saw her liberal opinions as evidence of mental illness, and since he believed in the viewpoint of eugenics, he strongly held that she should avoid passing the illness down to any other member of the family. Thus he was against her marrying and having children. It was as simple to him as that: Nell should remain single and childless. As one of her nieces remembered, Nell's father "ruined her aunt's romance," probably by convincing Chambers that she was—or would soon be—mentally ill (Leidholdt 54).

Her brothers too explained away her new liberal opinions and unladylike behavior—which they believed were just short of communistic—as manifesting a form of mental illness, calling her abnormal, eccentric, and irresponsible. One of her brothers, Kemp, who ran a textile mill in Durham, wrote to his father, "I think that Nell's method of living is not only improper, but highly dangerous. I think it is extremely risky for her to come home late at night, and I would not be surprised any time to hear some distressing news in connection with the same." He concluded, "She is evidently insane." Another brother, Dick, who also worked in the textile industry, was distressed by his sister's "disconcerting level of independence" and attributed it, again, to her "disordered mental state" (Leidholdt 57).

Lewis might have been depressed after her father's interference in her romantic life. Her biographer, Alexander H. Leidholdt, has suggested that she suffered from bipolar disease, but if so, it had nothing to do with her views of the possibilities for women in the postsuffrage years. She was certainly not alone in her opinions about independence and women during the 1920s and 1930s.

Lewis persisted in defying her father at every turn. One day in 1920, with a string of vehement disagreements with her father perhaps weighing on her mind, she left her father's house, mounted her horse, and galloped toward downtown. Passing the offices of the *News and Observer,* she stopped and impulsively applied for a job. She must have made a startling picture, flushed and windblown from riding her horse and wearing her riding pants and boots. Little did she know at the time how this one seemingly random act would determine the path that the rest of her life would take. She was hired by the newspaper on the spot and initially directed to write about the new "Women's Age" of the 1920s, but she impressed her editor so much that she eventually found herself reporting on state politics as well as strictly women's issues. In 1921 she began her column, "Incidentally," which she would write for decades and through which she would influence generations of North Carolinians on politics, social issues, the criminal justice system, labor, and cultural life.

Despite her family's disapproval of her public opinions, she took up causes such as women's rights, workers' rights, and civil rights—becoming one of the first southern journalists to capitalize the "N" in "Negro." Tensions within her family flared when she became embroiled in a labor dispute at a textile mill in Gastonia, a town near Charlotte. Despite her brothers' positions in textile management, Lewis spoke out on the part of labor through her column. When the strike elevated to violence and eventually led to a murder trial, she began to devote more and more space to convincing the public that labor was in the right. Through her column she managed to keep the defendants from being railroaded. She later campaigned to free imprisoned members of the union. Her involvement in this dispute helped establish her reputation as a defender of justice for the underdog and a voice of liberalism in North Carolina.

While Samarcand—strictly for white girls—was being built, she wrote in favor of a parallel institution for black girls, knowing all the while that she would probably be opposed. Such were the prejudices against teenaged black girls that no one was ready to put the tax money into such an institution. It took decades for black adolescent girls to be considered anything but sexual temptresses who were simply wired that way.

Her father's death in August 1926 no doubt triggered feelings of regret that their relationship had been so combative, but it also offered her financial security that added immensely to her self-confidence and independence. She used part of her inheritance to study law at Columbia University, hoping to use the practice of law to further her fight for the underprivileged in society.

She ran for a seat in the General Assembly of North Carolina in 1928 but lost—a defeat that relieved her brothers, who were embarrassed by her candidacy. They feared that their own reputations would further suffer if she officially moved into politics, as it would thrust her into the spotlight where, they believed, women should not strive to be. Despite the loss, she continued her fight through other means for progressive ideals, including her advocacy of many organizations that fought to help the less fortunate in the state of North Carolina. In the 1920s she served as director of publicity for the State Board of Charities and Public Welfare, and she was the first vice president of the Committee on Women in Industry of the North Carolina League of Women's Voters and eventually served as president of that organization. She was secretary of the Central Commission to secure a survey of women in industry in North Carolina and a member of the North Carolina Historical Commission.

In 1929 Lewis edited a report on capital punishment in the state, considered a landmark study of the system, looking at twenty-six cases of death-row inmates and analyzing the race and socioeconomic standing of each inmate between 1909 and 1929. In one of her columns, she called capital punishment "our official slaughter record" (*News and Observer,* February 3, 1935). She also wrote an article in the *Public Welfare Project* condemning those who would execute criminals who are mentally defective. She argued that "a large majority of the criminals who are sentenced to death in the State, about half of whom are executed, are mentally defective; a number are definitely insane; while others have psychopathic tendencies. . . . The clever, the rich and the influential are not found among those whom we condemn to die" (10.4 [1929]).

By the time the Samarcand fires occurred, hers was a name the public knew and respected. With her law practice, she hoped to pursue justice for a variety of less fortunate citizens of the state, and her inheritance made it possible for her to defend the Samarcand Sixteen for only a nominal fee—although her father would have been shocked and appalled that his money had been put to this cause. Her brothers continued to believe she was mentally ill and that her action of taking on the case was clear evidence of it. While she did suffer from occasional bouts of depression that left her unable to work, she was a long way from "insane."

In the spring of 1931, just a few weeks before the fires at Samarcand, Lewis proudly opened her law office on the sixth floor of the North Carolina Bank and Trust building less than a mile from her new house and St. Mary's, a school that was quite a contrast from the institute her future defendants would be accused of burning down. Despite the privileged life Lewis had led, her progressive ideas empowered her in the role of defender of the poor white girls involved in the Samarcand fire. She felt she had an understanding of the girls, even with their class difference. She read of the girls' frustrations with their housing and treatment at Samarcand, and she was reminded of the women's movement to get the vote. In fact she had once written that to advance women's rights, "a few parades, some heckling, a smashed window or two and a little arson" might be necessary (Pyron 70). What the girls had done may not have been smart, she knew, but it certainly got people's attention, and that was always the beginning of any change.

She did not hold the girls' class against them. Although, like most southerners, she "sanctioned racial purity," she also warned her readers that eugenic policies could be twisted and abused by those in power. Her brother Ivey was a staunch believer in eugenics, and her stand only increased the rift between them: Ivey was a member of the Anglo-Saxon Club in Virginia, whose goals were "nearly identical to the Klan" (Leidholdt 88). She wrote in her column that eugenics was worthy of consideration, "but it seems to me that there is lots of dynamite in all this talk of Nordic supremacy. It is becoming the sort of thing that sows the seeds of war. Witness the way the Ku Klux Klan, of course one of the greatest social menaces at present, has taken up the refrain" (Leidholdt 89). Eventually she claimed that she no longer believed in "chosen people" (Leidholdt 90).

Lewis was appalled by what she read in the papers about the girls and blamed McNeill for not giving them better advice. She was disturbed by the image the press was creating because she knew that for the girls to get leniency and justice, public opinion had to be on their side. From the experience of writing her column, she knew that the public could be swayed easily, but one needed to know how to do it without appearing to do so.

Inmates exercising on the grounds of Samarcand Manor. Courtesy of the State Archives of North Carolina.

So far the girls had been presented as wild and untamed, the result of no parental guidance and bad home environments. They were portrayed as ignorant and licentious, sirens luring young boys away from good homes. The reports depicted the girls as immodest, scantily clad vixens smoking cigarettes and posing for the cameras.

Samarcand was not faring much better in the press. Lewis had done a piece on the training school a few years earlier for the paper, and from her brief examination of it she had given the school good marks for organization and discipline. However, it was receiving no such accolades in 1931. An early false report from the *Elizabeth City Daily Advance* shockingly claimed that "sex perversion or sodomy is practiced in each cottage and all inmates are paired off as sweethearts—one being a boy and one a girl—and that they love each other in that relationship" (April 22, 1931).

While Lewis did not know everything that went on at Samarcand, she knew that the superintendent, MacNaughton, would never allow such scandalous behavior at her school. Most of what had been published in the papers so far had been rubbish, Lewis suspected, and part of her defense would include a campaign to change the information released and therefore alter the perception of the girls.

The one positive thing she read was that the jailer in Lumberton, Mr. Austin Smith, seemed to have become a father figure for the girls. The Lumberton paper noted, "Under the fatherly guidance of Jailer Austin Smith, the girls have learned to like the Robeson county jail and Lumberton. They prefer to remain here, many of them say, and would like Jailer Smith as their keeper always." But Smith would eventually show himself to be no match for these rambunctious girls. Their sentiments toward him would drastically change in just a few short weeks.

Coincidentally, one newspaper story that caught Lewis's eye was about Stonewall Jackson Training School for Boys in Concord. On the same day that the Samarcand Sixteen had burned down two buildings, two boys at Jackson had burned a pair of cottages there. The boys, Edward Eggers and John Durham, claimed to have been severely beaten by the instructors of the school and so burned down the cottages in retaliation. Eggers confessed only, he said, because he was whipped until he did so. He implicated Durham, he continued, only to make the whippings stop. The school officers, of course, claimed that this story was untrue. Similarities to the case at Samarcand would become obvious as Lewis began to study the facts and to interview the girls and other witnesses. The boys' trial was set for several weeks before the Samarcand trial, so she would watch with intense interest how it was handled and what punishment the boys would get. It could set a precedent for the Samarcand Sixteen.

Meanwhile, Lewis set her course for the next few weeks. She planned to visit the girls in the Robeson County Jail, and she needed to find witnesses for the defense. Most important, she needed to develop a defense strategy.

THREE

When Lewis visited Carthage on April 24, her first interview was with Virginia Hayes, whom she was hired to defend. In addition she met with the other six girls at the Moore County Jail—Marian Mercer, Rosa Mull, Dolores Seawell, Josephine French, Wilma Owens, and Margaret Pridgen. Her goal was simple: learn about the girls and their backgrounds; start to get a sense about their motivation in starting the fires; and then give them some advice about speaking to newspaper reporters. No doubt she was hoping that knowing the girls would help her construct a defense that would sway the courts to their side.

The stories were all heartbreaking ones of girls coming from homes without both parents or in some cases without any parent. Poverty, disease, and ignorance seemed to be major themes of the girls' lives. Lewis took copious notes about each girl, noting age, physical characteristics, birthplace and family, education, illnesses, sexual history, date and reason for commitment to Samarcand, and any stories told about life at Samarcand, as well as whether the girl had confessed. She even included specific quotations from the girls. She typed up all the notes when she got back to Raleigh and cataloged her findings. Her organization probably helped her determine which girls to put on the witness stand and which girls would not make the impact she desired.

She learned from Virginia Hayes that Hayes was born in Rocky Mount, in eastern North Carolina, and lived for a while in the piedmont towns of Leaksville and Walkertown. She was a rarity in that both parents were alive and together, although her mother was listed as "Sick." Having four younger siblings probably meant that she had had to help with their care, a reason why, Virginia said, that at age sixteen she was in the sixth grade—although school records showed her as in the fourth grade. Before being sent to Samarcand six months earlier, Virginia had run away from home because her father "fussed at her." She had fled to Greensboro and stayed at a boardinghouse and, she admitted, "got to running with bad girls." Although she denied having sex, the "bad girls" she mentioned were most likely a reference to sexual activity. Like so many young poor girls her age, it was her sexuality that got her into trouble, and Virginia's official records at Samarcand listed a charge of prostitution and labeled her as "very bad." The welfare office at Reidsville committed her to Samarcand.

When Lewis asked Virginia if she liked being at Samarcand, she answered with a resounding "no," further explaining that the people there "just treat you terrible—gave us horse beatings—make the girls fire the furnace." She added that she "had to sleep on one blanket on the floor" and would rather be in jail than back at Samarcand. About the fire, she claimed that she was out in the yard when the first fire started in Bickett and was in bed when the blaze began in Chamberlain Hall. She told Lewis that Miss McClary would not open the doors of the girls who were locked in, despite a blazing fire, but finally gave the keys to a girl to do so. This probably sounded improbable to Lewis because, as this was her first interview with one of the girls, she had no idea what life in Samarcand was really like. Wild young girls creating imaginative stories, she perhaps thought.

Lewis asked Virginia why she confessed when she did not start the fires. She told Lewis that she did it with the thought that it would get her out of Samarcand and on her way home. She had recently received a letter from her father saying that her mother was sick and asking if she could come home. Miss MacNaughton had refused to allow her to go. On the night of the fires, Virginia claimed, she had words with MacNaughton, who—according to Virginia—did not ask them but rather told them that they had started the fires and should confess. Virginia had sassed back, "Well, if I've got the name to bear, you can think what you please."

Virginia's story was not so different from those of the other six girls housed in the Carthage jail—all between the ages of thirteen and sixteen. Of the six, only two had both parents alive, although one of the mothers lived in a home for the insane; two lived in a one-parent home; and two had neither parent alive. All came from large families and lived in poverty. Education was low among the girls—most around a sixth-grade level. The two who had been given IQ scores were listed as "feebleminded." All six had become sexually active early, Wilma Owens having lost her virginity the earliest, at age eleven. Therefore it was not a surprise that all six were brought to Samarcand with the charge of "running around," a code phrase for being sexually active. One girl, Marian Mercer, had a mother who, before she died, had run a brothel.

Girls swimming in the pond on the grounds of Samarcand Manor. Courtesy of the State Archives of North Carolina.

The girls recounted tales of whippings, being locked in a room for as long as six months, and harsh teachers who called them "gutter rats" while they were at Samarcand. Dolores Seawell had her hair cut off for trying to run away, and several others who had run away from Samarcand were chased by bloodhounds. All who had run away had eventually been returned to the facility. The files at Samarcand, to which Lewis eventually had access, listed five of the seven as "very bad" and one, Josephine French, as "immoral and disobedient." Despite MacNaughton's statement that all of the girls had confessed to starting the fires, only three in this group claimed they actually did. One of those, Rosa Mull, told Lewis that in truth she had had nothing to do with the fires but pretended she had in hopes of being sent home. All of them wanted out.

At first it was probably hard for Lewis to believe that such punishments occurred at a state school with such a good reputation as Samarcand had. She had heard similar stories of girls being stripped bare and made to lie on the ground while teachers took turns using the whip on them, up to one hundred lashes or more. But as the interviews continued and the stories told were so similar, she had to start believing. Samarcand was not what people believed it to be.

She was also distressed that four of the seven girls, Virginia Hayes, Josephine French, Wilma Owens, and Margaret Pridgen, had told her they had received appendectomies while at the school or during their confinement in prison. What she did not realize at the time—and what she may never have figured out—is that girls were often sterilized under the guise of an appendectomy or other minor surgery. North Carolina law limited sterilization to three classes: psychotic, epileptic, and feebleminded, but to get around that, places such as Samarcand had other means. In a 1949 article called "Sterilization and Social Welfare: A Study of Current Developments in North Carolina," Moya Woodside—in her enthusiastic support of eugenics—wrote that "social agencies in the desire to lessen some of the many problems presented by continued fertility, ill-health, and poverty, often turn to sympathetic surgeons who will interpret 'therapeutic'" sterilizations "in the broadest sense of the word" (205). In fact a doctor did not even have to recommend someone for sterilization: North Carolina was the only state to allow social workers to designate people for the surgery.

State institutions in North Carolina often labeled sterilization "therapeutic" rather than "eugenic" to avoid involving state officials. They simply reported that the patient's health depended on the surgery—such as a patient having appendicitis, which was one of the most common surgeries that involved sterilizations, so much so that sterilizations were nicknamed "Mississippi appendectomies" (Cahn 174). Did these four girls, and at least two others in the group in Robeson County, all really have appendicitis while at Samarcand? Such suppositions are difficult to confirm since school records from 1931 did not indicate individual sterilizations. What we do know is that between 1929 and 1947, 75 percent of the 1,901 eugenic sterilizations in North Carolina "were performed on females, half of whom were between the ages of ten and nineteen. Samarcand was one of the main cooperating institutions among various state schools, submitting at least three hundred inmates for sterilization" (Cahn 67). Of the 1,901 cases, 1,260 of the victims were labeled "feebleminded."

A few days after her first interviews in Carthage, Lewis set out for Lumberton, the county seat of Robeson County about one hundred miles south of Raleigh, to continue her interviews. The jailhouse, a plain two-story stone building with a center tower, looked imposing. Inside, the walls were a dirty beige with ugly green tile, and the concrete hallways were narrow, almost claustrophobic. After introducing herself and explaining she was the new lawyer who would defend the Samarcand girls, she was shown to a room for meeting inmates. If she had been allowed to see the cells, she would have been appalled at the girls' accommodations: cells barely big enough to hold four girls in each, with plain cement benches and hard cots.

The stories she had heard in the Carthage jail continued with the nine girls in Lumberton. Large families, poverty, missing or dead parents, and a fourth- to sixth- grade education had limited the choices for these girls. They had ended up in Samarcand for "immoral conduct," "running around with boys," "prostitution," or merely being in danger of prostitution. Nearly all admitted to having sex early in their teens and finding boys an escape from their limited and usually miserable lives.

To Lewis, the girls did not seem feebleminded. In describing Mary Lee Bronson in her personal notes, Lewis wrote, "Pretty, attractive blond, apparently of good intelligence. Pleasant and courteous manners. Tall and slender. Looks as if she might well be at St. Mary's." About Edna Clark, she noted, "Pretty, spirited, rather bold brunette. Quite attractive. Medium height. Much interested in everything. Evidently sociable. Pleasant and polite manners." Yet "feebleminded" was what most of these girls were called, a label put unduly on them for their lack of public education, their lack of social graces, and their lack of the advantages in life that other young girls had been given. Since they had been largely unprepared for the kinds of questions asked on the IQ test, low scores should have been expected, and other ways of interpreting intelligence would have been fairer. But as each girl entered Samarcand, the IQ test was administered, and "feebleminded" was more often than not the resulting description.

The stories of whippings, beatings, and solitary confinement continued from this second group of girls. Edna Clark claimed that she was whipped three times, one time so severely that she had to be taken to the hospital and "painted." She said that five teachers at a time had whipped her. Estelle Wilson remembered that they would "lock me up every time I turned around" and were planning on whipping her the day after the fire. Pearl Stiles had been whipped with a leather strap and knew of beatings so severe that "they would put water in their faces to keep them from fainting." Mary Lee Bronson was sent to the discipline hall merely for being rude to a teacher.

Of course all of them were described in their permanent records as incorrigible. Edna Clark was "very bad," and Ollie Harding exhibited "all kinds of delinquency." Mary Lee Bronson was listed as "beyond parental control" and "attitude not good." The nicest things written about a few of them were "not so bad" and "not so good."

One girl stood out, though, as different from the rest. While all the stories were sad to Lewis, Margaret Abernethy's was tragic. Margaret's father took her away from her mother when she was just four years old, and Margaret never saw her again. She had no siblings. Later she was told that her mother was dead. Her father remarried a woman who raised Margaret along with several half siblings. She had an uneventful childhood until she was ten years old, when her father began to molest her sexually three to four times a week, always when her stepmother was out. She did not tell anyone because, she said, "It was against my will. He kept me scared." Her stepmother seemed to know nothing about the molestation until one day when Margaret was about thirteen. In Lewis's notes, she quoted Margaret's words: "My step-mother had just had a baby and he slipped down to my room and she caught him there that night. After she found out, my daddy told me he was going to kill me, and I ran away and went to a lady's house not far off. They got the police and carried him to jail. Then they took me to the county home. I didn't like it there and I would run away. Then they carried me to Smithfield to a Mrs. Crump's who kept children for the welfare people." He was not molesting her while he was drunk; in fact, Lewis noted, "Father drank, but was not drunk when he mistreated her, she says." When Lewis asked if Margaret ran around with boys, she claimed, "I never ran around with boys; he wouldn't let me." Lewis added, "After he [*sic*] father's conviction, she was sent to Samarcand." There she had been for the past three years, simply because the state did not know what to do with her. She was a victim, and yet she was locked up, whipped on four different occasions, and told that this treatment was for her own good.

Of these girls, only three said they confessed to the fires; the rest denied it vehemently. The ones who confessed, Edna Clark, Thelma Council, and Margaret Abernethy, all said they did it as a way to get out of Samarcand. But it was the girls' words versus the words of the officials at Samarcand. Whom would the judge believe?

During the week following the interviews, Lewis wrote several letters to other lawyers whom she had heard were going to represent other individual girls. She had heard from one of Virginia Hayes's siblings that the family was going to hire a Winston-Salem lawyer, and from a different source she was told that another lawyer would be representing Margaret Pridgen. Neither was true, and Lewis was again at the lone helm of the case.

After Lewis's initial interviews, she wrote several letters, the first one to George McNeill. She recounted her findings and suggested that the real crime in this situation was in the treatment of the girls at Samarcand. This, she believed, could be a major part of the defense—that the girls were merely defending themselves against an unjust system and participating in what could be called civil disobedience. It was, after all, an American ideal that anyone had the right to rebel against an unjust system; the country had been founded on such a principle.

The second letter was to Dr. Harry W. Crane. Crane was a professor of psychology at the University of North Carolina at Chapel Hill and a member of the State Board of Charities and Public Welfare, specifically the Bureau of Mental Health and Hygiene. He had been a well-known expert in criminal psychology since writing his first article on the subject in 1912. Lewis explained to him her defense of the girls and her suspicions about the mental capabilities of some of them. If they could be shown to be mentally defective in some way, along with being underage, she might be able to get them released or at least get their sentences reduced. He wrote back and agreed, saying that the examinations of the sixteen cases would take between two and three days. With such a time commitment and with the trial approaching, he said, "I am not sure at the present time just when I would be able to go." He suggested that some of the girls might have already been examined and that she should check the records. Lewis responded with the offer to pay him for just four of the girls: Margaret Pridgen, Marian Mercer, Margaret Abernethy, and Pearl Stiles, as they were most at risk for receiving punishments because of their blatant confessions. Lewis and Crane set up a tentative date for the examinations.

Next she wrote to Mrs. Janie Carlyle Hargroves in Lumberton, a woman she had learned about from the sheriff in Robeson County. Mrs. Hargroves had expressed interest in helping the girls in prison and suggested that there were other women in Lumberton who felt the same way. Lewis introduced herself and thanked Mrs. Hargroves for her interest in the case and then asked if she "and the other interested ladies in Lumberton" could make sure that the girls, "when they appear at their trial," would be "dressed as neatly and as modestly as possible, so that they may make a good impression in court." Impressions were important, Lewis knew, and having them dressed like young ladies rather than paupers would send a message that they were like any other girls their age.

Last, she wrote to the sheriff of Robeson County, P. S. Kornegay, and thanked him for his kindness when she was in Lumberton. She commended him, Jailer Smith, and the "good people of Lumberton" for their "interest in and kindly treatment of the Samarcand defendants." In conclusion, she said that his treatment of the girls "made me feel that my clients are in excellent hands." This note is surprising, considering what had happened just a week earlier. Frustration had been building among the girls at the Lumberton jail.

The initial interest in their case had waned a bit, and the newspaper reporters were not coming around as often. The girls were getting low on cigarettes, and they were starting to feel abandoned—by the public, by their families, and by Smith, the jailer, who would not allow them out of their jail cells often enough to suit their tastes.

On April 22, when they had been in one prison for almost six weeks, some of the girls began banging objects against the bars of their cells and shouting to be let out in order to listen to some music, and soon other girls were joining in the protest. Smith heard them but ignored them, having had about all he could handle from these impudent girls. At first he had been mildly flattered by the interest he got from the press and the reporters who wanted to ask him questions, but once that attention disappeared, all he was left with was nine girls who demanded more and more of his time. The more he gave them, the more they seemed to want, and he barely had time for anything else because he was running around trying to find the things they asked for: matches, cigarettes, magazines and newspapers, and even hair ribbons.

When Smith refused to let them out, they decided that if fire had worked once, it might work again. Carefully they stuffed newspapers under their mattresses and lit them on fire. The paper caught easily, and the old mattresses on the cots were not far behind. Soon smoke was wafting throughout the jail. "Fire! Fire!" all the girls began yelling. Jailer Smith came running. Terrified at seeing the smoke and flames, he quickly began unlocking the cells and letting all the girls out into the hallways. The girls spilled out of their cells and realized they were completely free because Smith was busy trying to put out the fires. They could not actually leave the jailhouse, since it was locked with a key that Smith carried with him, but they could have some fun in the rooms that were available. They began running throughout the jail, kicking and throwing anything they could lay their hands on: chairs, desks, books.

They threw chairs at the windows, breaking them, and overturned tables. They rifled through drawers and found pens and sharp pencils, pocket knives from former prisoners, cigarettes, and matches. They yelled, cursed, and created chaos while Smith beat at the mattresses with blankets to put out the fire. Even after he managed to extinguish the flames, he could not control all the girls at once, and he found himself at their mercy. If he cornered one girl to try to talk her back into her cell, a crash would come from the next room and send him scurrying to find out what had happened. No one came to help because at first no one knew what was happening.

The riot continued for several hours, even after help arrived in the form of the sheriff and his deputies, who had seen the broken windows from the street. Several of the girls surrounded Smith, the deputies, and the sheriff, and they jabbed the air with knives and shards of glass to keep them at a distance. The girls acted like cornered cats using their claws and teeth to defend themselves. They threw plates and glasses and books at the men, who cowered, unsure about what to do with such violent young women. The men had been taught to show women respect, and that included not forcing the girls physically to get back into their cells, so the girls continued to break furniture and destroy anything that stood in the way of their freedom. The men tried to stay out of their way and let them use up their energy until they were too tired to continue tearing things up.

By the time the sheriff and his men realized they could not stop the riot without getting physical with the girls, hours had passed. Eventually physically restraining the girls was their only recourse, and gradually order was restored. Girls were locked back into their cells, interviews were conducted, and the instigators were separated, but the girls did not seem to care. They were in the spotlight again.

When word about the Lumberton riot reached Lewis, she was frustrated. Her words to the girls about behaving to improve their reputation in the press had apparently failed to make an impression. In despair she realized her case was hanging in part on the behavior of girls who were young, frustrated, and desperate. She had hoped the public—and the judge—would pity them, but the girls were doing their best to turn opinions against themselves.

In the Carthage jail things at that time seemed to be quieter. Only seven of the girls were held in Carthage, and the jailer, A. W. Lambert, seemed at ease. Despite the girls' recent activities in Lumberton, Lambert seemed to believe that he could control his own inmates. The jailer imagined perhaps that the account of the Lumberton riot was exaggerated or that the jailer in Lumberton was inexperienced and inept. Mrs. Lambert, a sweet and gentle woman, told the girls that they would be treated with respect and expected that no trouble would occur. She believed that giving them tasty food and letting them listen to music on her Victrola would encourage them to behave. The jailer and his wife were wrong.

On the afternoon of April 30, six of the seven girls in the Moore County Jail were agitated. Virginia Hayes, their friend and fellow inmate, had been taken away for an appendectomy. They were restless because the jailer's wife had not come to let them out of their cells that day. Bored and looking for something to do, pacing in their cells, talking to each other, and occasionally calling out for attention from the jailer and his wife, their frustration mounted. They looked forward to being released each afternoon, getting to talk to one another, listening to music, and expending some of their teenage vigor; their pent-up energy was nearing explosion.

At about four o'clock in the afternoon, their frustrations reached a peak. Since they had been behaving well so far, the jailer had given them cigarettes with matches, never believing for one moment that his jail was in danger. But it was. All of the girls except Margaret Pridgen, who refused to participate, stuffed magazine pages under their mattresses and set two cots on fire. Then they started yelling and screaming, "Fire! Fire!"

Jailer Lambert appeared and ran through the hallways with his ring of keys releasing the girls from the smoke-filled cells. Then he ran to his office and called the fire department after he saw that the job of putting out the fires was beyond what he could do. While he continued to run frantically between the cells and his office, the freed young women ran through the hallways breaking windows, leaning out to look at the people on the street, and as the *Moore County News* reported, keeping up "a continual stream of verbal vulgarity, curses, and imprecations . . . at the top of their shrill young voices." Eventually several hundred people, alerted to the action by glass falling from the windows, gathered around the jailhouse and watched the spectacle of the swearing girls, the rushing firemen, and the frantic jailer, sheriff, and deputies.

The faces of the girls showed every bit of anger they felt. Their hair was wild, and their eyes were flashing. On April 30 the *Moore County News* reported that with their "faces, mostly pretty, distorted with rage, clothing disheveled, hair awry and eyes gleaming, they seemed to be angered to the point of temporary insanity." The fire was quickly extinguished, and all calmed down. Then an hour later the sirens were heard again, and as the *News and Observer* reported, "a fire of some proportion had been started and it took several minutes to get it under control. Just when the excitement was at fever heat, the crowd was horrorstruck to hear the news shouted that a bunch of the girls had cornered Clint McCaskill, one of the firemen working on the second floor, and were slashing him to ribbons with their knives." The newspaper further reported that "the six girls had armed themselves with pocketknives they obtained from a container in which personal belongings of prisoners are kept. They threatened volunteers who brought the hose inside the jail and McCaskill was stabbed in the melee." The truth was not quite so dramatic; McCaskill was only verbally assaulted, and the sole mark on him came from a shard of glass from one of the windows he had broken himself. He was quoted in the same article, though, as saying that he thought his "time had come."

The men were baffled. They had no idea how to contain and restrain these wild and unruly girls who were still on a rampage in the jailhouse, and even though there were only six of them at the time, it seemed like more. In desperation, Sheriff McDonald gave an order to the firemen, who turned the hose on the girls: "They were given a good drenching and this quieted them. New mattresses were placed on their bunks and they were locked up again in their cell, this time with the smoke." The sheriff and his men must have been frustrated, although McDonald's words to the *News and Observer* on May 1 were quite diplomatic: "Sheriff McDonald says the Samarcand girls are troublesome, but he has not despaired of getting them reconciled to patiently waiting for their trial. 'They are not vicious' he said. 'They do not really want to harm anyone. Setting fire to the bunks is just a prank with them. Of course, if they were men, we would know how to deal with them. But we cannot be rough with them. We shall continue to be firm with them, but at the same time to be as kind as they will let us be.'"

Meanwhile the *Moore County News* reported on April 29 that "the other nine girls, still held in the Lumberton jail, have evidently caused the jailor there no further trouble as he has not registered any complaint with the local authorities." Apparently he was no worse for wear from their "all-night riot, in which the faces of some of their kepers [*sic*] were scratched and a plate was thrown in the face of Solicitor Tom McNeill, and during which many window glasses and much furniture was [*sic*] broken."

Lewis received the news of the Carthage riot in a letter dated April 30 from George McNeill, in which he said he found the girls incorrigible:

> I went down to the jail, and they were acting like raving maniacs, smashing and breaking windows in the run-around, and perfectly nude. It was necessary to call out the Fire Department, and turn water on them in order to subdue them.
>
> These girls here do not have sufficient mental capacity to act right, and take the advice of the people who are trying to help them.
>
> Dr. Symington, Rev. J. H. Buffalo, and several of us, have talked to them, and they promised to be good prisoners, obedient, and not use any indecent and profane language, but continue to disregard and break all promised. I am afraid that about all we can do for them, will be to get them in the Criminal Insane Department of the Penitentiary.

By the time she received this letter, however, Lewis had also read the newspaper report and was trying to become more philosophical about the girls' behavior and take into account their frustration. She wrote back to McNeill on May 2 agreeing that "they are very troublesome and embarrassing clients, and one is much tempted to lose patience with them," but in her heart she felt for them, realizing their frustration and anger at the system that had failed them. Why would they not misbehave? After all, behaving well had not gotten them anything they wanted. If the stories the girls had been telling of the beatings and other punishments at Samarcand were even half true, she knew that in their place she probably would have done something equally desperate to make her case heard. She remembered all the struggles of the women's movement to get the vote, and she recognized a legitimate rebellion when she saw it.

Despite what seemed like another setback, when she went through the articles recounting the second riot, she noticed something different in the tone of the newspapers. For some reason the press was not blaming the girls as often or as severely for their behavior as she would have expected. Instead journalists were blaming the girls' circumstances. Along with the kind words by Sheriff McDonald, on May 7 the *Moore County News* described their actions as "the outpouring of emotions long pent-up; a demonstration against the treatment which they have been accorded by society." The newspaper seemed to justify their actions: "Highly emotional, with the energy and longings of just girls, they bear confinement just so long when they must do something to break the monotony of the darkened jail cells with bars and walls to hold them in."

Another story, this one an earlier editorial by Kate Ford Peele in the *Elizabeth City Daily Advance* published on April 22, was highly sympathetic toward the girls. Despite their bad behavior at times, Peele wrote, these girls were not "fiends incarnate" but rather were "like girls everywhere. They respond instantly to kindness, and if they get restless in the springtime and seek their freedom in a foolish way, that starts them on the road to great restrictions and punishment, isn't that just human nature after all? Girls outside of institutions do foolish things in the springtime, too." She went on to describe the girls as "merely underprivileged and neglected. Most of the worst ones haven't done a thing that they couldn't get by with gracefully and easily were they in 'high society.'"

The May 2 edition of the *News and Observer* contained an interview with one of the girls, Josephine French, in which she told her story as she remembered it. She claimed that the girls thought they had been forgotten and started the fire merely "to bring somebody up to let us out." She remembered that the firemen did not turn the hose on them but rather that they got "wet as drowned rats" because "they were putting out the fire." About the knives she said, "There were only two girls [who] had knives and they wouldn't cut. We didn't try to fight anybody. We just wanted to get out of this room for awhile [*sic*]." The article went on to characterize them as a "group of average high school girls. . . . They were fresh and bright . . . dressed in clean, brightly colored print dresses, stockings rolled to the ankles . . . overflowing with energy, all trying to talk at once, hesitating, and then beginning again, the group of girls who have figured on the front page for several weeks might walk into a high school class room and not be different from the average. . . . They were unanimous in their opinion that they 'wouldn't have my mother see my picture in the paper for anything.'"

The girls were beginning to be seen as the victims they were, Lewis believed, and they were depicted as young adolescents, not fully grown adults. She hoped the judge too would see the girls that way. Annette Louise Bickford, in an essay on the legal ramifications of the trial, saw the change in opinion to be a key element and one that had to do with North Carolina's publicly choosing its national identity as either part of the barbaric South or part of the civilized greater world: "The changing perceptions of the defendants from 'wanton slatterns' evoking racial otherness to guileless children was [*sic*] clearly influenced by popular negotiations of national identity, and would in turn influence the outcome of the case. Lewis' justification of the girls' actions as defensive rather than defiant came to be generally applauded by the public, who overwhelmingly supported Lewis as she went to trial" (454).

A letter dated April 30 arrived for Lewis. It had been penned by Kate Ford Peele, the woman who had written an article in the *Daily Advance*. Peele said that there were some things she could not use in the story because they were from a friend of hers who had worked at Samarcand and she wanted her to remain anonymous. Her words shed some light on the characters of the girls as well as the young woman who had taught them briefly:

> The young teacher was devoted to her girls, believed them to be just as good as plenty of other girls she knows and then some, and quite as good as some of the people who have them sent there, and, as she thinks, thus perhaps started them on the wrong road. One girl of the nine facing the serious charges, she thought was sent there for a very

> trivial reason by a girl much worse than the Samarcand girl. She tried being good at the institution and couldn't see that it paid, so went on a tear and tried being bad, getting in much deeper than she had ever dreamed. She thought the girls who set the cottages on fire were not abnormal or depraved but, like most girls their age, did not look ahead to vision the results of their act.

After the riot, the rest of the girls at Moore County Jail began to ostracize Margaret Pridgen, who had resisted participating in the riot and tried to talk the others out of setting fire to the cots. Through letters from her grandmother and discussions with Lewis, Margaret had started to realize the severity of her actions at Samarcand and the possible results of her confession, but the other girls held her new attitude against her. The harassment of Margaret by the other girls became so severe that the jailer moved her to a separate cell on the first floor of the jail. Her grandmother wrote to Lewis about the move, confessing that Margaret "is easily influenced by older girls" and so being away from the other Samarcand inmates would be best. She went on to write that Margaret claimed she was praying constantly to be set free—as was her family—so that they could bring her home "and train her in a Christian way."

One especially hopeful note of the week came with news about the boys involved in the Jackson Training School fires. Edward Eggers, who was only fifteen years old, had pleaded guilty to setting the fires but was given only a one-year penitentiary sentence. The other boy, John Durham, who claimed he had never confessed, although this was disputed by the school official, was released. Since arson was a capital offense in North Carolina in 1931—meaning that the electric chair was a possibility—this was good news for the Samarcand Sixteen. The boys, like the girls, had told stories of whippings, including the whipping of Eggers until he confessed. The precedent had been set, Lewis hoped, for light sentences, if any.

A few days later, on May 2, the topic of the Samarcand Sixteen was again the lead story in the state's newspapers. The *News and Observer* reported that the state legislature had passed a resolution stipulating that if the girls were sent to prison, it must be the state penitentiary because at least one section—death row—was fireproof. One senator had argued against the resolution, stating that the "State Prison was a fire trap and the girls would be a danger to hundreds of convicts," but the other senators were so worried about the girls burning and rioting again in the jails at Carthage and Lumberton that the resolution passed. Two senators, one from Moore County, added that "if the girls were not taken out of the Moore county jail, there was no telling what would happen." It was extraordinary the extent of influence these young girls had—even though they had no idea how they were affecting society's institutions all the way up to the state legislature.

FOUR

On November 20, 1926, Lewis had published a newspaper article about Samarcand, and as she reread it in preparation for the trial, she recognized that her opinion had been based on a rather cursory examination of the school and its superintendent. In the article she praised the superintendent, MacNaughton, for being a "modest and efficient" woman who "attends to her business admirably without any hullabaloo about it." About the school she had written, "The most striking thing about Samarcand is the good spirit which pervades the institution and for which Miss MacNaughton is chiefly responsible" and that "it has every appearance of a well-run boarding school." She praised the institution, remarking that it "is one of the State's most efficiently run institutions and received gratifying praise from authorities outside North Carolina who know what an institution for delinquent girls should be."

This had been purely a superficial conclusion, and Lewis knew it was time to get the story straight for the trial. Was Samarcand a well-run institution of learning and compassion or a hellish prison? She wrote to Agnes MacNaughton on April 30 and introduced herself as the counsel for the defense. She announced her plans to visit Samarcand on May 4 and asked for a tour and interviews with both staff and students. On May 3 she heard from MacNaughton that she would be welcome to come.

Lewis took the train to Southern Pines, passing from the urban bustle of Raleigh to the countryside of farms and small towns and finally into the sand hills of North Carolina. The area was dotted with peach orchards and stands of pine trees—beautiful in its own way—but the small communities she passed through were clearly suffering from the Great Depression. Each town, it seemed, was poorer than the one before, especially along the railroad tracks. Small shanties had sprung up, and groups of men, standing or squatting in circles, were doing nothing but waiting for times to get better. The sky was a beautiful Carolina blue, though, and many trees and bushes were flowering in the warm spring—a stark contrast to the poverty that was enveloping North Carolina and the nation.

She did not have to wait long at the station before a car from Samarcand arrived to drive her to the school, a distance of just over twenty miles over mainly gravel and dirt. After almost an hour of bumpy roads, the driver turned off Highway 70 and drove another three miles. An ominous sign saying "State Property. No Trespassing" and "Park Outside the Gate" might have given Lewis the impression that this was not a place where visitors were welcome. In fact her driver told her as he walked her through the wrought-iron gate toward the main building that visitors were generally allowed in only one day a month between 1:30 and 3:30 in the afternoon. All conversations were to take place under a guard's watch in a specific room designed just for that purpose or occasionally—if the weather was nice—outside on the lawn, but still under guard. Lewis hoped she would have more leeway than that with her visit.

As she walked along the gravel path toward the administration building, she could see various groups of girls, most of them wearing brown knickers with white blouses and brown ties around their necks. Here and there, though, she saw girls in identical outfits but blue instead of brown, a designation, she knew from her interviews with the girls, of a girl who was being disciplined. Girls were pulling weeds in the gardens, feeding chickens, riding in wagons, and hanging out laundry. All appeared peaceful on this day, but Lewis knew that under the surface, another reality might exist. She promised herself that this time she would wait to form an opinion until she had more facts.

Miss MacNaughton met them at the steps of the administration building, called "The Manor," the original house for the family when it was a working plantation. It was an imposing structure, meant to impress and intimidate, with eight white pillars lining the front of the building and additional wings of the house spreading out on both sides. For a few years before World War I, it had been used as a private preparatory school for boys, but the war forced its closing, and the state was able to buy the whole 224 acres for a mere thirty-five thousand dollars and instead use it as a girls' training school. Agnes MacNaughton had been its sole superintendent since then, having had some experience running other correctional institutions in the Northeast.

She was a no-nonsense woman who would not have smiled or waved as Lewis approached. Her posture alone sent a message of discipline and control as she stood at the top of the stairs with shoulders back and hands

May Day celebration at Samarcand.
Courtesy of the State Archives of North Carolina.

crossed in front of her body. Lewis realized that MacNaughton probably knew that the girls had told her stories of their lives at Samarcand and had prepared herself to contradict those tales.

MacNaughton, as usual, attempted to be completely in control of the interviews, and Lewis got a sense that the women she relied on most heavily were devoted to her and would do anything to keep things at Samarcand as they were. When Lewis got home, she listed the people she had talked to as "Dramatis Personae," suggesting that what she had seen was a performance of a kind. She included the names of Miss MacNaughton, Miss Stott, Miss Crenshaw, and "Possibly Miss Bradshaw and Miss Scurlock and Miss Ross" as "The Ring," alluding to an almost sinister gang of women who would keep each other's secrets.

First Lewis met with MacNaughton, who told the story of the night of the fire much as it had been reported in the papers. Lewis took copious notes. According to MacNaughton, "All [were] eating supper (about 6 o'clock) when the blaze in Bickett was first seen from Tufts. Betty Robinson, president of student council, who had been in her room sick, told Mrs. Moore, matron of Bickett, and Mrs. Moore got girls out in perfect order." She continued with a speculation that the fire might have come from a spark. When Lewis asked her if Pearl Stiles had anything to do with it, MacNaughton replied, "She doesn't acknowledge it. . . . I warned them to say nothing if they were not guilty." Lewis questioned why Pearl was sent to jail if she did not confess, and MacNaughton responded that a girl named Hilda

Godley, who was in the same room with Pearl that night, claimed that Pearl confessed to her. MacNaughton then told Lewis that there was a rumor that the fire in Bickett was to be a signal to the other girls to start their own fires.

She went on to give details about the fire in Chamberlain. Apparently, she stated, one girl went around to the other girls and announced that there was going to be another fire. The attic door was locked, MacNaughton affirmed, so she was sure it had been started by shoving "fat pine and rags through the ceiling." Who did it she was not sure, since the girls from Chamberlain were in the yard. The second fire started, she said, in four different rooms, but when Lewis questioned her about which rooms, she said simply, "I don't know." She admitted that some girls were locked in their rooms when the fires started but said that there were five women on the floor with them and that they eventually got everyone out safely.

MacNaughton went on that when the girls were brought to her after the fires were safely put out, "The first thing I said to them, 'You must remember that if you had nothing to do with the fire to stay out of this,'" and she instructed those who did have something to do with it to go into the teachers' reception room. She claimed that all of the fifteen defendants who stayed in Chamberlain went in. Lewis then recorded some specific and important points in her notes, some quoting MacNaughton:

> Claims positively that she did not question them individually and privately one by one.
>
> "My idea was to save the rest."
>
> "All I was thinking about was to get the dangerous ones off the ground."
>
> "Several girls said 'I did it.'"
>
> "Miss Ross spoke to the girls."

According to MacNaughton, Miss Stott, Miss Ross, and Miss Markham were present when the girls were questioned, although in her notes Lewis typed a question mark next to Miss Markham's name. Then Lewis asked about punishments for wrongdoing at Samarcand. MacNaughton must have been ready for this since she knew the defendants had all talked to Lewis. She claimed that extra work was the main punishment but admitted that the punishment depended on the crime. When asked about the sixteen, she responded, "Only two of these defendants, I think . . . had corporal punishment." Lewis knew this was a blatant lie, having talked to the girls. She asked for the names of teachers who had left Samarcand right before or right after the fires. MacNaughton reluctantly gave her six names.

A parlor at Samarcand Manor.
Courtesy of the State Archives of North Carolina.

Next, Lewis interviewed Mrs. Moore, who had been at Samarcand for about six months. She gave much the same story but added that Pearl Stiles had been late to dinner and that she had more demerits than any other girl. Her names of the group of women who were in on the questioning were a bit different: Miss MacNaughton, Miss Stott, and Miss Ross, but Miss Crenshaw instead of Miss Markham. She also mentioned that Sheriff C. J. McDonald attended the questioning the next day.

Miss Ross, the matron of Chamberlain Hall, was Lewis's next interviewee. She told Lewis the same story about the fires. Lewis wrote in her notes that when asked if she had been present at the initial questioning, "Miss Ross denies that she was present when girls were officially questioned. Note that Miss McN. says she was." Ross also denied being at the questioning the next day but claimed that Miss MacNaughton, Miss Crenshaw, Miss Stott, the sheriff, and "other men" were. By this time Lewis was wondering just who was where when questioning took place. What witnesses were there when the girls all confessed, especially since so many of them had denied to Lewis that they had been there? When asked about punishments at Samarcand, Miss Ross claimed, "We always try reasoning and persuasion. Corporal punishment is administered with a switch—never use anything else now—used to use leather."

Lewis then interviewed Miss Stott, who came prepared with her own notes. Stott listed five girls who were sent to prison the first night and said, "They were all together in Miss MacNaughton's office," meaning that they were not questioned individually. Then she offered a list of twelve names and said, "These have all confessed to me to actually setting the buildings on fire." Her last list contained three names, the ones who "have confessed to knowing about the fires."

One name on the last list was Pearl Stiles, the girl who supposedly confessed to her roommate later that first night, saying, "We set it on fire." When Lewis asked Stott who "we" referred to in the sentence, Stott gave her three names that Lewis had not heard before: Lettie McCraw, Ruth Crexy, and Leda Deweese. MacNaughton later told Lewis, "This is the first I've heard about that." When pressed by Lewis, Stott admitted that Pearl had not actually confessed to her that she had set the fires but confessed only to knowing something about them. Stott hurriedly added that Pearl Stiles and Ruth Crexy would not do their duty and "sing" that night but rather suspiciously "laughed and giggled."

Stott continued, "I warned the girls that it was a capital offense and that they should be careful," and Lewis noted carefully beside this quotation, "She knew that arson is a capital crime." Last, she asked Stott about punishments, to which Stott replied, "They don't average a whipping once a month and never whip a girl for one offense." Stott believed that only two of the defendants had been whipped: Margaret Abernethy and Edna Clark. Lewis must have interviewed Miss Crenshaw as well—although there are no notes—because she wrote the following next to Stott's names: "but Crenshaw said three [including] Josephine French (?) or Marian Mercer (?)."

Clearly enough discrepancies existed among the stories that Lewis knew someone was not telling the truth. When her interviews were finished, she was efficiently escorted back to the waiting car and driven to Carthage, where she would spend the night and catch the train the next day. That night at the Carthage Inn, George McNeill met with her, and she filled him in on the interviews and the suspicions she was developing. On May 6, she wrote to George McNeill more about those suspicions and reported, "I have today received information relative to the administration of Samarcand which confirms me in the suspicions I had when I visited the institution, i.e. that something is very decidedly wrong there. I am practically sure that the authorities there are very much disturbed at the idea of being called to the witness chair at a trial, with the consequent danger of disclosure of the internal trouble at the institution." She ended the letter with a promise to fill him in on what she had learned.

The information she mentioned came as a result of a dozen letters she had written to employees and former employees when she returned home from her visit to Samarcand, employees whose names and addresses she had gotten from Miss MacNaughton and the other women. Most of Lewis's letters of inquiry said the same thing:

> As information regarding conditions at Samarcand Manor may prove to be very important in the defense of these unfortunate girls, I am trying to gather all the facts I can, preparatory to their trial.
>
> I understand that you formerly were connected with this institution, and I shall be very much obliged to you if at your earliest convenience you will write me of your impression of the situation there, and especially whether you knew of any trouble between the Superintendent and members of the staff. Also, I particularly wish to know your opinion of the method of punishment employed at Samarcand.

She also wrote a note to Miss MacNaughton thanking her for the "courteous reception" when she visited and asking for copies of her most recent biennial reports. Now she just had to wait for replies from former employees—and hope that people would be honest.

Letters, dated just two days later, began arriving, as did an actual person: Lottie Mitchem, a former teacher at Samarcand who lived near enough in Raleigh to go to Lewis's office. Mitchem had started working at Samarcand in September 1930 and left only five months later, in February 1931.

The first question Lewis asked her once they settled into the interview was why she left so soon after being hired. Mitchem, looking nervous, said that she "had to make false reports to the county superintendent (of education) to the effect that no girls in the school were absent or tardy, when they were." When Lewis asked for clarification, Mitchem explained that Miss MacNaughton liked a perfect school and wanted the records to reflect that the school was run efficiently and the girls were well behaved. If a girl was absent from a class, for example, a teacher was not allowed to mark her as such. All the girls were to be marked present in class, even if they were in the hospital or locked up in their rooms.

Lewis then asked her about her impression of Miss MacNaughton and her inner circle. Mitchem professed that she was intimidated by her boss and believed that the administrators "have been there too long. They are too old.

Samarcand inmates on a wagon.
Courtesy of the State Archives of North Carolina.

They are not fair to the girls or teachers. I think this can be seen easily by the fact that a great number of teachers stay there only a short time. This past week, the doctor, the nurse, a hall counsellor and principal resigned because of the mistreatment they had received from Miss MacNaughton and Miss Tobbit." She maintained that teachers never knew from one minute to the next what the rules were and what was accepted as proper behavior at the school. Everything could be satisfactory one day and the next be all wrong. She claimed that one day she reported two girls, Margaret and Mary, absent and was praised for her accuracy. The next time she reported an absence she was criticized. The teachers were all rather bewildered by this type of learning by trial and error.

Lewis next asked her about punishments at the school, and Mitchem dropped her voice in response. She asserted that she had never actually witnessed a whipping but that other teachers and some of the girls had told her about the corporal punishment. "Everyone knows about it," she offered, describing the process Lewis had heard about from so many of the girls: a girl would be taken to the discipline hall, made to lie down on a rug, and held down by other girls while she was whipped by several teachers in succession, using "sticks and leather belts." "I heard the girls screaming several times from my building (Bickett)," she explained, "and once I heard them screaming when I was in the school building." Those who did the whipping, according to Mitchem, were Miss MacNaughton, Miss Crenshaw,

Miss Stott, and Miss Ross—with Miss Beavers responsible for whipping the smaller girls.

Mitchem told of specific stories she had heard, such as that of Ludie Draughn, who told Mitchem she received 250 licks one time and 300 another. A different girl—currently at the State Prison Colony for Women—was whipped several times in one week. Josephine French too was severely whipped, and Pearl Gibson was said to be so black and blue after her whipping that one teacher fainted at the sight. The rumors were all over the school, Mitchem insisted, and it was hard not to believe them when they were all so similar. In addition she claimed that one girl became so overwrought after her whipping that she tried to kill herself, an act that was hushed up.

Mitchem went on to discuss other problems at Samarcand, such as diseased girls locked up with healthy girls and overcrowding in all the halls. She alleged that in the discipline hall the blankets were never washed, so whatever one girl had would be passed on to the next. She also reaffirmed what the sixteen girls had been telling Lewis about roaches and all sorts of insects, especially in the discipline hall. The Honors Cottages were in need of adequate bath facilities, with separate areas for diseased girls. More clothing was needed, and there was also "need of better co-operation between Miss MacNaughton and workers."

Mitchem blamed the administration for most of the problems. She believed that the school could be saved, but only if many changes were made, including the end to corporal punishment and exposure to disease, and of course a change in administration: "We need a Superintendent there who would not allow the girls to be beaten unmercifully or unnecessarily exposed to those venereal diseases and who would co-operate with the teachers in the welfare of the girls." When Lewis asked her if she would be willing to testify in court about what she had said about Samarcand, Mitchem hesitated but agreed. With just a few changes, she believed, the place could really be excellent—maybe "one of the best in the state."

Soon after Lewis concluded her interview with Lottie Mitchem, she began receiving letters from former employees of Samarcand. The stories were all similar, and with just a few exceptions they were all critical of the school. As each letter came in, Lewis put together a list of possible witnesses for the defense, knowing she would have to whittle it down eventually.

Georgia Piland helped prepare meals from October 1930 to January 1931 before her frustrations became too much and she left Samarcand. She, like Lottie Mitchem, noted that Miss MacNaughton gave no specific instructions to any teacher, "but should we fail to find out and do the things expected we

Some of the youngest inmates at Samarcand. Courtesy of the State Archives of North Carolina.

were held responsible." Workers never knew what was acceptable and what was not. When she first arrived, she asked for a meeting with MacNaughton but was told by Miss Stott that "it might be two weeks, but that she would let me know when she wanted to see me." The superintendent also refused to offer a contract to any teacher or staff member, retaining the right to dismiss anyone at any time—which she was known for doing quite often—and giving the fired workers only fifteen minutes to get their belongings and leave, without ever telling them what they had done to deserve dismissal.

Regarding her job preparing meals, Piland felt that the money was spent unwisely: too much on starches and sugars and "too little [on] fruits." Georgia, like Lottie, had heard the screams of girls being whipped many times but could do nothing about it. She wrote in her letter dated May 9, "Upon two occasions while I was there I saw long whips or switches carried in Chamberlain Hall by Miss Stott, Sec. to Miss MacN. Miss MacN was at the door when she carried them in. Soon I heard screams and was told by the girls in my kitchen that they were whipping one of the girls. One would judge the whips to be either black gum or hickory, and they looked to be from five to six feet in length. It was not two or three whips, but a great bundle of them."

From October 1929 to March 1931 Dr. C. W. Durham had served Samarcand as its physician. He wrote that he had given "my service gladly and did not get thank you." He confirmed what Lewis had heard from Georgia Piland's letter: that Miss MacNaughton had no set rules and regulations, no meetings with the staff, and no suggestions about how to improve. He felt that part of the problem was that MacNaughton was getting too old to run Samarcand: "I do not believe the place will ever accomplish what it should as long as she stays there unless she has regular meetings with the working staff. She has no rules or regulations and that is like a ship without a rudder." Dr. Durham told a story about going to the hospital one night to see a patient and finding a group of girls stranded there: "I found about 15 girls in the hospital . . . locked up and the keys up at the Superintendent's house, no one to look after the girls in case fire should have started. I know this to be the fact as I was called up there to see a patient." If a fire had started, he wrote, the girls would have been at its mercy and no doubt perished.

When Lewis wrote back to Dr. Durham asking if she could submit his letter in the trial, he wrote back with great hesitancy, "I rather you would not present my letter to the court as it might hurt my work here." He was currently working in Jackson Springs, North Carolina. "If I knew just what part you wanted to use, it would be different, but the whole letter would be passed around and I might need some further explanation." He went on to suggest that Lewis contact one or more of the nurses who had worked at Samarcand.

In fact Lewis already had received shocking letters from two nurses previously employed at Samarcand: Viola Sistare, who had worked there for eight months; and Bessie Bishop, who had been employed there for ten months. Both had the complaints of not being given directions and then being criticized for following their own inclinations. Sistare said she left "because I could not stand the continued interference of those to who [*sic*] nursing was a science they knew nothing of and their commands were of little or no sense—and if followed would have resulted most disastrously for the three hundred children under my care. I was allowed at no time to act under my own judgment and was ordered to change my reports and to alter them to please the whims of the reigning power." Bishop made a startlingly similar statement.

Sistare and Bishop, like Lottie Mitchem, had been forced to change records—omitting reports of dog bites and burns, for example, because they would reflect badly on the institution, and on Miss MacNaughton's dog, Jack, who bit the girls. Both of the women witnessed brutal beatings of the girls and then afterward tried to calm them and tend to their black and blue welts. Both nurses were asked to produce pills for the beaten girls to "quiet" them because the girls had become so hysterical that their conduct was distressing to others.

Facilities were abominable in the hospital: no chairs, broken beds, no windows, no linens or gowns, no toothbrushes or paste. Sick girls were housed with healthy girls, and sometimes sick girls were sent out of the hospital. When MacNaughton came to the hospital and found that a diphtheria patient of Bishop's had been isolated according to doctor's orders, she said, "'I don't care for Doctors orders, I will not stand for that at all.' And the child was taken out and sent to the playground with the other children." Sistare told one especially heartbreaking story:

> Speaking of locking the girls, I should like to cite one instance of the locking discipline. There is a child at Samarcand, a poor feeble minded creature, who has gonorrhea and syphilis. She has such a virulent form of halitosis and a very terrible body odor that it is impossible to stay in her direction long at a time. She practices all forms of masturbation upon herself and other children—teaching them practices they have never known of. These things were reported and Dr. Durham backed me in my request that she be sent to some place—for such a child. Instead she was disciplined and locked. When girls of the Manor needed a very grave measure of discipline—they were locked in a small room with this child. She is still in the institution and is really a menace, in more than one way to the other children.

When the nurses treated the girls for their wounds that resulted from the punishments they had suffered, sometimes Miss MacNaughton criticized them for lessening the girls' pain and told the nurses to "let them suffer they deserved it." Unlike the doctor, both nurses agreed to testify.

One hall counselor described life at Samarcand Manor as a "constant smouldering undercurrent of dissatisfaction" with a "lack of cooperation between teachers and the powers that be." The study rooms for the girls had no tables and poor lighting, making it nearly impossible for the girls to do any real work. This counselor left after seven months, she wrote, "after having had my intelligence insulted and my stupidity counted on as long as I felt I could tolerate it and still retain a shred of self-respect." She specifically objected to girls of various ages being thrown together in rooms so that young girls were exposed to what older girls talked about long before they

Girls' bedroom at Samarcand.
Courtesy of the State Archives of North Carolina.

were ready to hear such things. She also noted the falsified record keeping: "There is no school having a perfect attendance of 250–275 pupils, daily, for the school month. It is absurd, and an utter impossibility. And yet, Miss Lottie Metchem [*sic*] our principal of the High School, was told to mark them present, regardless." The counselor's complaints and stories continued for seven typed pages.

Several letters came from teachers who had been forced to leave Samarcand for reasons that were never made clear to them. The former athletic director thought everything was fine with her work, but she had suddenly been told she had fifteen minutes to get her things together and leave Samarcand. One teacher received a leave of absence when her grandfather in Virginia became ill and needed her care. However, when this teacher tried to return to Samarcand, Miss MacNaughton told her she had felt betrayed by her absence and accused her of lying about her grandfather's illness. MacNaughton refused to rehire her. Another teacher put things succinctly when she wrote that the administration of Samarcand "violates all the principles of psychology, sociology, and school administration." This teacher also supported the claims of beatings: "I heard sickening reports of how children were forced to lie upon their stomachs on a rug while beating[s] were administered with a strap. Some said these whipping[s] would last as long as thirty minutes, and consist of over some hundred licks. Teachers in Hope Chamberlain Hall, and all the children had to listen to this, while the recipient wailed and begged, groaned and sometimes swore. Who could blame them! On two occasions I saw Miss MacNaughton slap children over the head." She remembered that the beatings were so severe, two girls had to sit on cushions for two weeks afterward.

Still another former teacher reported that Agnes MacNaughton had "spies" within the school, creating an atmosphere that was "tense and unsettled" most of the time. She also supported the stories of beatings, having seen "big black and blue stripes across the back of a youngster about nine years old." Another teacher was fired without ever being given a reason and—like the athletic director—was given fifteen minutes to leave campus. She noted that the girls had "a good deal of uncertainty regarding the length of time they will be kept at Samarcand. I do not know whether the girls are told how long they are to stay in the institution or not, but some of them stay twenty-seven months, thirty months, or similar lengths of time, seeming to think they are staying overtime, and wanting to go home." Another teacher believed the girls to be "just like girls everywhere except perhaps a little more backward. In behavior they were cheerful, carefree, and [had] lots of what is called 'school spirit.' At times, however, they were very dissatisfied. They longed to go home." She summed up the plight of the girls with these words: "They are looked upon by some of the teachers as prisoners."

Letter after letter arrived supporting the claims that Lewis had come to believe were absolutely true: beatings occurred quite regularly; Miss MacNaughton was capricious with her discipline; the girls were generally good but untrained; the physical conditions were unsanitary; and many of the employees were frustrated and beleaguered. One interesting letter came from a former employee who said that Agnes MacNaughton's dog, Jack, was treated much better than any of the girls were. He—unlike the girls—was kept free from fleas and slept in the soft bed of his mistress, "the Queen."

Because of the publicity that Lewis's role as defense attorney had garnered, she also began to get letters from parents whose daughters had spent time at Samarcand. One parent who signed her letter only as "Citizen," and who had been doing some research of her own, claimed that if parents "raise a voice of criticism they will only make it harder for their own child and like the woman who came to Soloman, [*sic*] rather give up the fight than make it harder for their child." She related story after story of girls being punished and their reactions to it:

> Some of the girls were unable to lie on their backs for days after a whipping.
>
> Mary Horton was whipped for refusing to participate in the whipping of her friend.
>
> Elsie Louise Clinard, only six years old, was whipped repeatedly for bedwetting.
>
> Ora Stanley was whipped for owning a pair of tweezers.
>
> Mary Ellington, Louise Frye, and Delia Frazier attempted suicide after whippings they received for trying to run away.
>
> Etta Mae Jones and Mildred Butler had their hair cut to the skin for stepping outside their cottage when they had been told not to.

Lewis made note after note and became more horrified with each letter, but she also became more certain that the truest crime committed here was not arson.

In a letter to the *News and Observer,* another woman, identified as Mrs. Bettie Watte but asking to be identified merely as "Citizen," wrote, "I am not prejudiced against the institution or its officials but as a citizen of the state feel my share of responsibility in attending any necessary house cleaning. But I can't do it without help." She titled her letter "Smoke Signals from Samarcand Manor" and began by telling the story of American Indians who were "taught to use rising smoke with a language more convincing than eloquent modern orating, to bring their tribes en masse into action gliding silently through the forest." She went on to equate the smoke rising from the fires set by the girls to these smoke signals, sending their message of abuse and mistreatment: "Let us forget the blazing headlines and think of the smoke from this fire as it rises carrying heavenward on and on through the clouds the thought and despair and helplessness of these girls who were locked within the walls of Chamberlain Hall" (May 6).

She continued by describing the way the girls in the disciplinary halls were restricted in meeting their families: they had fifteen minutes only, outside, "under escort or guard and they stand in the cold and timidly gaze while a few meaningless words can be said then they must part and that is as near as we get toward finding out what kind of place our child enjoys." She claimed to have witnessed these visits and told one story about a blind man whose daughter had been sent to Samarcand because she was helping him sell newspapers for money, an illegal activity. Her description was quite melodramatic: "They stood out in the road, she barefooted, and visited for 15 minutes with the officer completing the pathetic triangle till the 'times up' announcement was made. The father turned away and groped his way feeble and broken hearted and helpless, unable to read for himself the daily papers which he sells for his living." The letter writer continued by describing the switches used for beatings at Samarcand and concluded, "It is a wonder this institution hasn't burned long since from spontaneous combustion during one of these switchings."

Lewis gathered together all these letters, interviews, and newspaper articles and continued to work on her case. Meanwhile she was also corresponding with Dr. Harry Crane, the psychologist who had agreed to test several of the girls. On April 28 Crane wrote to Lewis suggesting possible dates for the exams: May 11, 12, 13, or 14. Feeling pinched for time, she wrote to him the next day selecting the earliest of the dates. He agreed in a letter back and also let her know, "We do not have examination records for any of the girls listed in the Samarcand records." At this point it seemed that Lewis planned to accompany him on his trip, but sometime between April 30 and May 11 Lewis decided to let him do the examinations without her. She requested that the sheriff at Lumberton and McNeill at Carthage see to it that Dr. Crane's interviews went well. Crane met Lewis at her office on the morning of May 11 and discussed the case with her before he left first for Lumberton and later for Carthage.

Harry Crane was a staunch believer in eugenics and supported the passing of various sterilization laws. North Carolina first passed such a sterilization law in 1919, as "An Act to Benefit the Moral, Mental, or Physical Conditions of Inmates of Penal and Charitable Institutions" designed "for the improvement of the mental, moral or physical conditions of any inmate of any of the said institutions." No sterilizations were performed under this law, however. Once the 1927 landmark decision of the Supreme Court upheld a state's right to sterilize its citizens forcibly, North Carolina legislators decided to try again. The 1929 law was titled "An Act to Provide for the Sterilization of the Mentally Defective and Feeble-Minded Inmates of Charitable and Penal Institutions of the State of North Carolina," and added to its role were the act of sterilizing "for the public good" and the mandate that no one involved in the sterilizations could be held legally responsible. Under this law forty-nine people were officially sterilized. This was the law in effect during the spring of the Samarcand fires and trials.

The law would be challenged and found unconstitutional in 1933 by the North Carolina Supreme Court and so was rewritten to create the Eugenics Board of North Carolina, which would oversee the operations and make sure that due process was followed. Harry Crane would become a member of that board and oversee many of the sterilizations that would follow in subsequent years. One of his fellow board members was R. Eugene Brown, who would write an article in 1935 explaining and defending eugenic sterilization in North Carolina. It is summarized briefly here to illustrate the philosophy that Dr. Crane endorsed. As the man who was to examine four members of the Samarcand Sixteen, his position is relevant. It is also significant that Brown wrote the mission statement for Samarcand Manor when it was opened in 1917.

Brown defined eugenic sterilization as "a means adopted by organized Society to do for the human race in a humane manner what was done by Nature before modern civilization, human sympathy, and charity intervened in Nature's plan." He believed that in place of the law of the jungle in which the strong would survive and the weak die, people had created a society in which "the weak and defective are now nursed to maturity and produce their kind." He claimed that public opinion was "most favorable to the development of a sound program of sterilization" and that such a solution "is far more important than the solving of any of the immediate problems of economic depression."

He went on in the article to explain the 1933 law and to whom it would apply: people such as "mentally diseased, feeble minded, or epileptic." He compared it to other laws in the United States that provided sterilizations for rapists, moral degenerates, and habitual criminals. Then he compared it to the German sterilization statute that legalized sterilization for hereditary conditions such as Huntington's chorea, blindness and deafness, alcoholism, and "serious hereditary bodily deformities." After giving numerous examples, he reminded readers that sterilization "is not a punishment; it is a protection" and records showed "that many moron girls paroled after sterilization have married and are happy and succeeding fairly well." Sterilization, he added, is "practical protection against threatened race degeneracy."

Brown blatantly stated, "None of the inmates of Caswell Training School"—the male equivalent of Samarcand—"should be released before being sterilized" because it was estimated that at least 40 percent were "feeble minded." He pointed out, "Out of 170 girls' cases studied at Samarcand Manor during the past year it was found that more than 50 per cent are definitely feeble minded." Statistically this seems improbable, and it suggests that the IQ tests being used on the girls were inadequate in determining intelligence, especially considering their backgrounds. Such IQ tests did not take into consideration that instead of being "feebleminded," these girls could simply be undereducated or even victims of trauma in their lives that would keep them from performing their best on the test. In fact many of the girls were physically or sexually abused, poorly educated, or just naive to the types of questions that might be asked.

"Feebleminded" was a label that threatened a person's life in many ways. Those labeled "feebleminded" "were believed to be the nucleus from which a wide range of social evils, including poverty, drunkenness, sexually transmitted diseases, and a range of other disability conditions, emanated" (O'Brien 7). They were "frequently described in the writings of eugenicists as diseased organisms, reproducing at an alarming rate and infecting the 'healthy' portions of the community" (O'Brien 33). For girls it was even worse to be labeled as such. In 1904 Walter Fernald claimed, "It is well known that feeble-minded women and girls are very liable to become sources of unspeakable debauchery and licentiousness which pollutes the life of young boys and youth of the community" (383). Sexuality became the sin that determined these young girls' reputations. Lack of intelligence was equated with uncontrollable sexual hunger. Since they were uncontrollable, "they required a degree of external control that other humans did not" (O'Brien 63).

Even doing well on the IQ test was no guarantee that a girl would escape being negatively labeled. One of the terms often used to describe girls of higher IQs was "dull normal." It implied that the girl could do well on an IQ test but might be unsuitable to live by society's rules. It was a loophole that allowed state officials to sterilize a possibly intelligent but poor and sexually active young woman.

Nell Lewis probably knew most of this when she sat down on May 11 with Dr. Crane to discuss the case, but she planned to use the philosophies of eugenicists to her benefit during the trial. It might have been no mistake that she hired Harry Crane to examine the girls and that she chose the specific girls she wanted him to examine. If she could prove that the girls were lacking in intelligence, that they were in a kind of childlike mental state, she could argue that they did not know what they were doing and did not consider the consequences of their actions.

Three days later Lewis received the results of his testing, and she was not surprised by any of it. He qualified three of the four girls as "'feebleminded,' and the fourth as a 'dull normal.'" He had ascertained that all four of the girls had IQs of less than seventy. Additionally he pronounced that the mental ages of the girls—despite being in their mid-teens—were all below age eleven. Lewis had her doubts about the legitimacy of the IQ assessments Dr. Crane had made since she had interviewed all of these girls and generally thought them to be normally clever but simply ignorant of social mores.

Crane had examined and tested Margaret Louise Abernethy, who was seventeen years and five months at the time, and found her to have a mental age of nine years and eight months with an Intelligence Quotient of sixty. Margaret Pridgen's chronological age was fifteen years and two months, but her mental age was eight years and ten months with an IQ of fifty-eight. Pearl Stiles, who was sixteen years and zero months, tested at nine years and nine months with an IQ of sixty-one. Crane found some inconsistency with the fourth girl, Marian Mercer. Marian stated that her foster mother, who took her in when she was three or four years old, told her she was fourteen the previous February 28, but according to her mother, who was living in Washington, North Carolina, she was sixteen on that date. Her mental age, however, was eleven years and one month. If she was fourteen years old, he explained, her IQ was seventy-eight; if she was sixteen, her IQ would be sixty-nine. These evaluations led to the inevitable and not surprising conclusion that Abernethy, Pridgen, and Stiles would be categorized as "feebleminded," while Mercer would be classified "dull normal" if she was fourteen years old or "feebleminded" if she was sixteen.

These complicated numbers were a tool Lewis could use in her case. She wrote to the judge and requested Dr. Harry Crane be called as a witness for the defense, and the judge agreed. By testifying that their minds were much less advanced than their bodies, Crane would help establish that the girls were too young mentally to understand the consequences of their actions—and that they certainly should not be tried as adults, as the state was doing. Lewis added this information to her trial arsenal.

During the final days leading to the trial, Lewis received letters of encouragement from women around the state who felt she was speaking not just for the Samarcand Sixteen but for all women who lacked a voice in society. Lisbeth "Polly" Parrot, the director of education and publicity for the North Carolina State Board of Charities and Public Welfare—a position Lewis had once held—wrote to her on May 1 expressing her support and encouraging her spirit: "This will be a new venture in social welfare in North Carolina, I believe. Don't get discouraged, please, for there will be many of us who are counting on you to bring to North Carolina a new way of looking at a child's meanness." Lewis wrote back thanking her and declaring that this trial "is just exactly that sort of thing that I want to do in my practice of law, and I am glad to be able to present the side of the delinquents at their trial." She admitted, "I have been sharply criticized for my connection with this case, but I am thoroughly satisfied about it in my own mind." She was happy to defend the girls because, she said, "these children have been greatly handicapped by society."

She corresponded with a woman who had taken in two foster children and had much advice to offer Lewis in her preparation for trial. The woman noted, "The Supt. of any reform school has a very hard place to fill and must be strict but I think they gradually and unconsciously become hard-boiled and lacking in charity." She admitted that "the girls are shallow and untruthful, sly and egotistical and have no standards and no proper background if they are like the one I had. Ready to shout at a revival or curse and fight as occasion arises." Lewis wrote back and professed that her position as defense lawyer was not easy: "I realized that, as you say, defendants of this sort are very trying persons to deal with, nevertheless, I feel very strongly that justice demands that these girls have their side of the matter presented at the trial as effectively as possible." Clearly Lewis was getting advice and opinions from many around her, some of it rather unkind; in one case it was suggested that she was betraying her own class by defending these poor white girls. But her belief in the system and in the absolute fairness of the law, along with her constant faith that she was doing the right thing, sustained her through the criticism.

She also received a letter from the mother of one of the defendants, Mary Lee Bronson. It was a cry of anger and shame from a woman who felt that much of what Mary Lee was being charged with was her mother's fault. She explained that she was a single parent and feared that Mary Lee would drop out of school too soon, so she thought that sending her to a "boarding school" would ensure that she finish high school. She herself had been an orphan, raised in the Masonic Orphanage at Oxford, and so lacked relatives or friends who could watch Mary Lee during the day and sometimes at night when her mother had to work. She did not want Mary Lee running around town unsupervised and heard that Samarcand was the kind of place where Mary Lee could become part of the community and blossom while she finished school. "Oh how badly that place was misrepresented to me," she practically wailed on the page. "I will never forgive myself for letting her go there." Lewis wrote back to her expressing optimism: "I believe it will be possible to show that your daughter, Mary Lee, was not implicated in the burnings. I saw Mary in Lumberton on April 28, and thought her a pretty, attractive, well-mannered girl. She told me, and I believe her, that she had absolutely nothing to do with setting fire to the Samarcand buildings. Of course, it is impossible to predict what the outcome of the trial will be, but I feel that Mary's chances are among the best, and you may be sure that I shall do everything in my power to clear her."

The girls were "Quietly Awaiting News of Their Fate," according to the *Moore County News* on May 7. After the riots, they seemed to resign themselves to being patient, although there was a "slight flurry Monday [May 4] when one of the girls again started a miniature blaze in their cell." The fire was quenched by Deputy Lawrence Kelly, with the help of some of the girls, "before it had gained any headway." The article went on to describe the routine the girls were following as they waited: "Every morning, under the supervision of the officers, the girls are released into the run-around and allowed to exercise. They romp and play like so many school girls, and seem to enjoy even this much liberty immensely. All seem more happy and carefree than one would think under the circumstances."

Just a few days before the trial was to begin, Pearl Stiles wrote a letter to Governor O. Max Gardner on behalf of the nine girls who were jailed in Lumberton. It was never delivered but was intercepted by members of the press, who published it:

> Dearest Governor Gardner, Will you please help us 9 girls in this case of trouble? We knew nothing at all about the burning of Samarcand Manor. Mr Garner [*sic*] the way we were treated is terrible. We were locked, beat, and fed on bread and water most of the time. Please give me liberty or death. We girls in Robisson [Robeson] County Jail, is just as innocent of this crime. They hold against us as a little child which has never known anything. Please pardon us 8 [*sic*] girls in Robison County Jail and help us to get out of that and trouble if you wish to. So we can go back home to our Parents those who have them, and the ones who hasn't any parents can be adopted out to people. Please give me liberty or death. If you will only help us out of this trouble we will be happy. Mr. Garner [*sic*] this is Pearl Stiles writing and I am always trying to be good I didn't have one thing to do with that old fire. Well all the girls said to give you their love for them. Will close with good heart. From Miss Pearl Stiles to Mr. Gardner. Lumberton NC. Answer at once.

When Lewis read this letter, she probably thought two things. First, despite having the power to pardon the girls, Governor Gardner would never do so. It would be politically risky to involve himself in this highly controversial case involving the death penalty and underage girls. If he pardoned them, he would be accused of showing favoritism just because they were females, but if he acknowledged the letter but did not pardon them, he might seem overly harsh. Second, Lewis knew that this letter would cement the public's sympathy on the side of the girls. No one could read this rather pathetic letter from a disadvantaged girl and not hope for her release and the release of the other fifteen. In fact a letter in the *Fayetteville Observer* published just before the trial claimed that Lewis and the girls "have the sympathy of ninety-five percent of all our people." Lewis became ever more hopeful that the court would be lenient.

Another letter came from a man who praised her for taking on the case. Like many people who wrote to Lewis, he saw the upcoming trial as a referendum on the justice system. "Perhaps this case may be instrumental in pointing a way to a saner method of dealing with society's recalcitrant members," he wrote. "Taken at its worst this is less the problem of delinquent girls than that of delinquent society."

Pearl Stiles's mother seemed to have little understanding of the justice system or of the seriousness of the charges brought against her daughter. She wrote to Lewis asking if Pearl could be excused from the trial and sent home so she could help care for the younger children while her mother worked, ending the letter with "I need her bad." No doubt most of the families of the girls had little idea of the possible serious outcomes of the trial. They were largely poor and uneducated, and the idea that their daughters might go to jail—or worse—just for starting a fire was unimaginable. Lewis knew that they did not understand the power structure and so thought that she could make some phone calls and make the whole thing go away. Their lack of understanding only added to her anxiety for this, her first trial.

In her final preparations for the case, Lewis presented her list of witnesses for the defense. She had decided to start with Dr. Crane and his analyses of the girls' mental capabilities, then bring on three of the former employees of Samarcand whom she had interviewed or received letters from: Lottie Mitchem, Georgia Piland, and Viola Sistare. Next she would bring to the stand eight of the Samarcand Sixteen: Margaret Abernethy, Edna Clark, Josephine French, Marian Mercer, Rosa Mull, Dolores Seawell, Pearl Stiles, and Ollie Harding.

Part Two

THE TRIAL

FIVE

In the state of North Carolina in 1931, first-degree arson was one of only four crimes that carried the death penalty. Arson, the definition read, "is the willful and malicious burning of the dwelling house of another," and to constitute the crime, four conditions needed to be met. First, there "must be some burning, though it may be slight." Second, "it must be of a dwelling house, or an outhouse used in connection therewith." Third, "the house must belong to another, at least as occupant." Fourth, "the burning must be caused maliciously." Perhaps the crime was considered so dangerous because in the past jailhouse burnings had been deadly. Recently, in a Columbus, Ohio, prison in 1930, 322 people had been killed in a fire set presumably by inmates.

Some flexibility existed, however. Since Samarcand was a school and not an individual's house, a different statute could apply: "If any person shall willfully set fire to any school house, or procure the same to be done, he shall be guilty of a felony, and upon conviction shall be punished by imprisonment in the State's prison or the county jail and may also be fined, in the discretion of the court." After Lewis engaged in some debate with the prosecutor, Don Phillips, it was this second crime that the girls were charged with—on one condition: that the girls all plead guilty to this lesser charge. Phillips, according to one newspaper account, "did not think society would demand that the State try the young girls for their lives" (*News and Observer,* 20 May 1931).

The pleas were entered, and the death penalty was off the table. Lewis could breathe a sigh of relief that a decision of whether the girls would live or die was not dependent on her winning. Because they were all charged together, they would be tried together in one trial. The *Moore County News* reported on May 28 that one trial "saved Moore county thousands of dollars." "Had the girls been tried for their lives," the story continued, "a separate trial for each of the sixteen defendants would have been necessary. That

Judge Michael Schenck. Permission granted by Ned Bittinger.

would have meant sixteen special venires [lists from which juries are selected] of 200 each. Jurors get $3 per day and mileage. Their pay, alone, would have been nearly $10,000 to say nothing of a hundred and one other items of expense." While this may seem petty on the county's part, it is important to remember that this trial took place during the Great Depression, and money was not easy to come by. The guilty pleas made it possible for the trial to take place in front of a judge—no jury—another move that saved money for the county struggling with finances. Since the verdict had already been decided, all the court was required to do was determine the sentence, and no jury was required for that. Everything depended on the opinion of one man.

That man was Judge Michael Schenck, a tall, stately man with wispy blond thinning hair combed back on his head. He was well respected, known throughout North Carolina as a fair and honest man. Schenck graduated from the University of North Carolina in 1897 and went to work with the American Insular Civil Service for two years in Cuba. He returned home and enrolled in law school at UNC, graduating in 1903. He first practiced law in Hendersonville and eventually became mayor of that small western North Carolina town. Married with one son and two daughters, he was appointed to a five-year term as solicitor in the Eighteenth District by

Governor Daniel Craig and prosecuted criminal cases in various counties in North Carolina. After World War I started, he served as a major in the Judge Advocate General Corps, never leaving the United States. After the war ended, he returned to law practice and was named superior court judge by Governor Cameron Morrison in 1924. Eventually he was elected to an eight-year judicial term, the position he held when he was asked to serve as the judge in the Samarcand case.

When Judge Schenck received the notice that he was to serve as the judge in the trial of the Samarcand Sixteen, he no doubt realized it was not an honor so much as a burden. It would not be easy to decide the fates of these adolescent girls. Judge too harshly and risk looking like a monster. Be too lenient and deny the seriousness of the crime—and open the door for other juveniles to commit serious crimes with impunity. Judge Schenck knew he needed to walk a tightrope in this case.

It would not be a long, drawn-out trial—it took place over just two days—because the girls had pleaded guilty. As the first day neared, reporters and curiosity seekers began to converge on the small town of Carthage. The case had received national attention, and journalists came from as far away as New York City to observe and report the proceedings. Without television, citizens relied on the coverage in newspapers, some published twice a day. The summaries of the action in court were described in detail, sometimes recounting the entire testimony of a witness, accompanied by all the reactions of those who had found a place in the courtroom. Reporters tried to bring the trial to life through the papers by describing in detail every word and gesture. Good reporting was considered an art in 1931.

The day before the trial, Lewis drove herself to Carthage and checked in at the Carthage Inn. She spent the afternoon with George McNeill going over their strategy. This highly publicized case was her first trial, and being nervous was probably a given. The fact that she was a woman only added to the pressure. At that time only 2 percent of lawyers in the United States were female, and she was only the second woman from Raleigh to try a case. Still, McNeill seemed to have turned over the responsibility of the trial to her, realizing perhaps that a woman defending girls would be seen more sympathetically by the judge.

The press was giving a great deal of attention to the case. The combination of an inexperienced woman defense attorney and the persistent image of the Samarcand girls as young, unruly, and sexually permissive made for great headlines and interesting copy. One newspaper, the *Southern Pines Pilot,* set the scene with a report at the end of the first day of the trial:

There were sufficient "features" to the Samarcand case to produce a best seller or pack a theatre, sordid as they were.

1. The crime charged was a capital offense.
2. The defendants were minors.
3. The defendants were pretty girls.
4. Woman was pitted against man as rival counsel.
5. Defendants had set fire to two jails during their incarceration before trial.
6. It was a trial of a State institution, a State system of caring for the delinquent children, as well as of the children themselves.
7. There was the element of suspense. Because of the previous uncontrollable conduct of the defendants there was no telling at what moment one or more of them might produce a scene.
8. There was the conflict of the protection of the public and the future lives of the children. They deserved State's prison. Would State's prison mean the ruination of those young lives? And if not State's prison, then what?

On the first morning of the trial, May 19, reporters seemed as interested in what the women were wearing and how they acted as in the legal proceedings. According to the *News and Observer,* Lewis arrived at the courthouse wearing "a gay cotton print" suit with a ruffled silk blouse, her hair bobbed and finger waved. She clutched her notebook and looked seriously—and a bit nervously—at the reporters and their photographers before heading up the stone steps. The girls arrived in their school bus, all wearing the dresses provided by the women of Robeson County. They linked arms and strode up the courthouse stairs together. They seemed to be treating the day as an adventure, waving to the crowd. With arms around each others' shoulders in solidarity, they stood for pictures. They smoked their last cigarettes, lit for them by reporters, on the steps of the courthouse before entering. Occasionally they hurled insults at reporters and photographers who got too close or who asked questions that were too personal.

The Moore County Courthouse stood in the center of the town on an island encircled by the main roads going in and out of Carthage. Three stories high, its stone walls were impressive and a bit intimidating. The county had built it in 1922, and the citizens were proud of its grand scale, feeling it gave their county a strength and solidity that could compete with any other in the state. Inside, the authority of the building continued with marble floors and a large stairway leading to the second floor, where the courtroom awaited.

Exterior of Moore County Courthouse.
Permission granted by John E. Deacon.

The courtroom was two stories high with two levels of large windows opened to catch the late spring breeze. Even the girls, usually so nonchalant and carefree, had to have been momentarily silenced and awed by the grand setting of their trial. On May 22 the *Southern Pines Pilot,* one of the newspapers that still serves Moore County, described the scene on the morning of the first day of the trial: "The case opened on Tuesday morning with the court room in Carthage crowded with the interested and curious, for not in recent years if ever has a trial in Moore county aroused so much interest. The sixteen girls, ranging in age from thirteen to eighteen years, marched into the court room looking much the same as any group of teenage girls, attractively dressed in silk and cotton dresses of various designs. Every one looked to be of reasonable intelligence."

The hardwood floors held twenty rows of bolted-down wooden benches, which were already filled by the time the girls arrived, with many more onlookers standing at the back and along the sides. Above the main floor a balcony seated black observers, many of whom had come from the country to see the spectacle.

Every eye in the room followed the girls as they took their seats in the second row, behind the lawyers' tables. People were intrigued to see the real girls they had been reading about for several months. In contrast to the larger-than-life images that had evolved by means of the press, the girls probably seemed small, even frail in this impressive room where their fates would be decided.

As the lawyers expected, few of the girls' parents or family members were present. Traveling from their home counties was expensive and time-consuming, and most probably did not understand the seriousness of the crime with which their daughters were being charged. For the most part, they were poor people with farms to run or jobs to perform. Some of their parents were dead, sick, or absent from the girls' lives for some reason, situations that had often led to the girls' discipline problems in the first place. Other parents had children at home who needed care, and bringing them to sit in an overcrowded, warm courtroom for several days was simply not an option. So most of the girls were essentially on their own, and this made them seem even more fragile. Since they had already pleaded guilty and were simply awaiting their fates, which would be determined by an inexperienced lawyer and a single judge, the suspense and drama of a normal trial were not expected by many. They would be wrong in that impression.

The eyes of North Carolina and much of the rest of the country were on the Samarcand Sixteen. Young girls on trial perhaps for their lives had caught the fancy of people everywhere, and the case had become more than just a trial about a fire. It had grown into a referendum about poverty, class, gender, eugenics, the prison system, and modern sexual mores. Many people believed that the stern backlash of prison crackdowns from the previous decade had gone too far and that prison reform was necessary. In the 1920s once prisoners were no longer hired out for income, prisons had fallen into decline because of this loss of revenue. They were dilapidated and overcrowded. In order to maintain control, guards sometimes resorted to abuse such as whippings and starvation. Many people wanted to see prison reform, and this trial would go a long way in convincing even more people of that.

The hum in the courtroom suddenly hushed as Judge Schenck was announced. The crowd in the room rose as one, men removed their hats, and attention turned to the man entering the room and who would decide the fates of these teenagers. The trial had begun.

Lewis and McNeill had agreed that the girls would all enter guilty pleas, with the exceptions of two of the girls, Mary Lee Bronson and Wilma Owens. The judge agreed. They were *nol-prossed* by the state: *Nolle prosequi* is Latin for "we shall no longer prosecute." It was deemed that there was insufficient evidence in the cases of these two girls, and so the Samarcand Sixteen became fourteen. Mary Lee Bronson would be sent home with her parents,

Interior of the main courtroom of Moore County Courthouse.
Permission granted by John E. Deacon.

both living, but Wilma Owens was an orphan. Lewis asked the judge what he intended to do with her. He answered, "I am going to place her in your custody." Lewis's eyes opened wide. She looked first at Wilma and then at the judge and replied, "But Judge! I don't know what to do with her!" "Multiply your problem by sixteen," he growled, "and you will have a conception of my dilemma."

After this exchange, which was captured by newspapers, it was time for opening statements. Solicitor Don Phillips gave his first. He stood up, and without leaving his place behind his table he began with a definition of arson and why it fit this particular circumstance. He mentioned that the *New York Times* had estimated the damages from the fire to be one hundred thousand dollars and that the *News and Observer* had figured double that. The insurance, he claimed, covered only thirty thousand dollars. He reminded the judge that the girls had pleaded guilty so it was only a matter of determining their sentences. His case was simple: they did it; they meant to do it; and they needed to be punished. He sat down. Then it was Lewis's turn.

Lewis stood and came out from behind her table and planted herself directly in front of the judge. She was a gifted writer who knew how to use words to create effect, and she used this skill during the trial perhaps as she never had before. She straightened up to her full five feet, four inches and began to speak. She read part of a poem by Rudyard Kipling to remind the judge that he needed to know and understand these young women and their upbringings in order to sentence them fairly:

> Ah! We judge each other harshly,
> Knowing not life's hidden force—
> Knowing not the font of action
> Is less turbid at its source;
> Seeing not amid the evil
> All the golden grains of good:
> And we'd love each other better
> If we only understood.

Then she quoted the lawyer and orator Robert Ingersoll from an address he delivered in front of the New York State Bar Association in Albany, New York, in 1890:

> We must take into consideration the nature of man—the facts of mind, the power of temptation—the limitations of the intellect—the force of habit—the result of heredity—the power of passion—the domination of want—the diseases of the brain—the tyranny of appetite—the cruelty of conditions—the results of association—the effects of poverty and wealth, of helplessness and power.
>
> Until these subtle things are understood—until we know that man, in spite of all, can certainly pursue the highway of the right, society should not impoverish and degrade, should not chain and kill those, who, after all, may be the helpless victims of unknown causes that are deaf and blind.

With the two prison riots—for which the courts had decided not to prosecute the girls—it was hard to argue that the girls were blameless. Lewis described the girls as unwanted by their own families and society—"human driftwood"—who were sent to Samarcand simply because no one knew what to do with incorrigible women who did not conform to the stereotype of the southern lady. In a chapter about the trial in his *Law and Society in the South: A History of North Carolina Court Cases,* John Wertheimer noted that Lewis "settled on a defense strategy that emphasized the traumas suffered by the girls before and, especially, after admission to Samarcand, thus evoking the sympathies of a paternalistic court without explicitly requesting favoritism for females" (445).

Lewis mentioned that a double standard existed for boys and girls who had done the same things. "Running around" was the "crime" so many of these girls had been accused of, but what was punished in women was tolerated in men. Lewis told the story of one girl who had done nothing wrong but who was sent to Samarcand simply for living in such environments that she was *likely* to develop into an immoral woman (Wertheimer 451). Alluding to a Clarence Darrow speech from 1924, Lewis went on to contend that sending the girls to prison would not be "merciful to civilization" because "if the law was administered without any feeling of sympathy or humanity or kindliness, we would begin our long slow journey back to the jungle that was formerly our home." She argued that people must transcend their baser instincts telling them to seek revenge and instead show mercy for the girls.

In conclusion she pointed out that not one of the girls had been sent to Samarcand for anything violent. It was only after spending time at Samarcand that these girls attempted a violent act. She quoted a line from an article in the *New York Times:* "The girls are apparently more corrupt than when they entered the institution." It was here that she began one of the main thrusts of her defense, and she spoke plainly. The real crime was what society and Samarcand had done to these girls. Arson was merely the self-defense of girls who had no other options but civil disobedience. They had started the fires, but they were the victims, not the criminals. Victims were not put in prison. They were helped to get over their trauma and encouraged in their attempts to get back to their normal lives.

She thanked the judge for his consideration and sat down. The prosecution called its first witness to the stand, Estelle Stott, secretary to Agnes MacNaughton and a member of what Lewis had identified as "The Ring" at Samarcand. Inexplicably, Solicitor Phillips had decided not to put MacNaughton on the stand, even though she was in charge the night of the fire. In a letter Lewis wrote to Kate Burr Johnson just a week later—which she labeled with the words "THIS LETTER IS ABSOLUTELY CONFIDENTIAL"—she reflected on this move:

> The trouble, I think [with Samarcand], undoubtedly centers in a Miss Stott, Secretary to Miss Mc Naughton [*sic*], who for some curious reason appears to have pretty well got control of things down there. As you will note, Miss MacNaughton [*sic*] herself did not take the stand during the trial, but the State depended for its main testimony for conviction on Miss Stott. When I visited Samarcand about two weeks before the trial, Miss MacNaughton [*sic*] told me with her own lips that she could not say that any one of the defendants were guilty. It was chiefly on their alleged confessions to Miss Stott that they were convicted.

> The thing is this, Mrs. Johnson: The institution now seems to be run by a small ring headed by Miss Stott who is supported by Miss MacNaughton [*sic*] in what seems to me to be a very odd way,—that is, I don't understand how Miss McN. has let this girl get so much power. This ring appears to have set up a petty dictatorship which has made the atmosphere of the place apparently so full of uncertainty and caprice that neither the "out" teachers or the girls know what to expect from one day to the next.

Whatever the reason, MacNaughton sat stoically near the prosecution table with her lips clamped tightly shut throughout the trial.

Stott, though, seemed extremely sure of herself as she recounted the official version of the story. In line with previous accounts, she testified that the first fire was reported to her between 5:00 and 5:30 P.M. and that by the time she arrived on the scene, the girls had been taken outside to the grounds. As the building was in its final stages of being consumed, a second fire broke out at Chamberlain. That one was quickly put out, but two hours later another fire completely destroyed Chamberlain. She also claimed that a few hours before the first fire, a storeroom had been broken into and boxes of matches had been stolen. One of the girls, she said, "had threatened to burn the hospital and had matches in her possession."

When Lewis cross-examined Stott, she began by asking about how and when punishments were meted out at Samarcand, but Phillips jumped to his feet and objected. He claimed that since it had nothing to do with the fire, it could not be presented as evidence. Lewis objected of course because much of her case depended on setting the scene of a brutal and violent place that led to the girls' rebellion. But the judge agreed with Phillips and told her she must confine her questions to what each individual witness had experienced.

Lewis then asked Stott to relate how punishment was given to the specific girls on trial. Stott admitted that at times girls were whipped with switches—much like their own mothers would have used, she asserted—and that the girls were made to lie on a rug on their stomachs to make the whipping easier. The *Southern Pines Pilot* summed up her testimony in the May 22 issue: "She [Stott] denied ever having whipped a girl while angry, and brought out the fact that the girls were not punished for running away, but for such infractions as tearing out window screens, using vile language and raising disturbances. She told of the system of sending girls to honor dormitories as a reward for even two or three days of good behavior."

Lillian Crenshaw, supervisor of the student government, was called next. Yes, she told Solicitor Phillips, she had been present at the questioning of the girls and heard several of them admit guilt. During her questions to Crenshaw, Lewis probed at length about the modes of punishment doled out at Samarcand. She asked Crenshaw to describe in detail the various punishments she had seen or been a part of, at least concerning the girls who were on trial. Crenshaw claimed that she specifically remembered none of the girls getting punished. She admitted, however, that girls did not have specific rules to follow and were therefore sometimes punished for crimes they did not know even existed. When Lewis asked her if hair cutting was ever done as punishment, Crenshaw claimed that she had heard of it in the past being done to girls who had attempted to run away but that it had not been done since she had been at Samarcand. Dolores Seawell, seated behind the lawyers, whose hair was just growing back from one of the shearings, told a different story just from her presence.

The only other witnesses for the prosecution were girls from Samarcand, sixteen-year-old Hilda Godley and fourteen-year-old Helen Wiggins. Hilda claimed that she heard a confession by at least one girl the night of the fires and so had told the authorities this. "It was my duty and I did it," she announced. Lewis asked her if she had ever been whipped as punishment for something she had done wrong, and she answered, "When I needed it, and I thank Miss McNaughton [*sic*] for it now." Helen testified that she had heard rumors of severe beatings but believed the stories were highly exaggerated by girls who liked to create dramatic tales of their lives. The prosecution rested, and the first half day of the trial came to a close.

During the lunch break, Lewis consulted with George McNeill. Lewis was worried about the judge limiting her to the girls on trial to make a case against Samarcand. She had planned to have the girls tell stories of terrifying beatings, hound dog chases through the sand hills, starvation diets, and all manner of horrors at Samarcand. Now she would be forced to make her case with just the stories of these specific girls, and she worried that the judge would see their accounts as prejudicial. After all, they were on trial for their freedom, and it would be easy for him to believe that their personal stories were highly exaggerated.

After lunch the girls marched in, still in high spirits and seeming to enjoy their temporary fame. Several waved to members of the press, and one blew a kiss before they turned and sat in their seats. They seemed content with the proceedings and did not show signs of fear or emotional breakdown. Perhaps, reporters suggested, they did not fully understand the seriousness of the charges against them. It was difficult to know since the press had been denied interviews with the girls since the beginning of the trial. The *News and Observer* described on May 21 how the girls were isolated by the court: "A deputy was stationed at the main entrance to the courtroom each time the girls were transferred to or from the room, the deputy being given orders to arrest anyone who attempted to pass through the door, while spectators were ordered to keep their seats until the girls had filed from the court, down the steps and through a cordon of deputy sheriffs and court attaches to the waiting school bus which conveyed them to and from the jail."

Nell Lewis began her defense by calling Dr. Harry Crane to the stand. As an expert witness in all things psychological, he had examined four of the girls. His testimony was essential in showing the girls as incapable of realizing the consequences of their actions, so Lewis felt that having him speak first would establish a professional authority for her case. She needed Dr. Crane to paint the girls as mere children causing mischief but not realizing the danger in which they put others. He sat in the witness chair with authority and seemed at ease as he glanced at the judge and then the audience. He was a professional man who was confident in his opinions and findings, and he had testified many times before.

No doubt Lewis would have established his credibility by announcing his positions in the state as an associate professor of psychology at the University of North Carolina and the psychiatrist to North Carolina on the State Board of Charities and Public Welfare. According to the *News and Observer,* he "testified that he had examined four of the defendants and that their mental ages were: Margaret Abernethy, nine years and eight months; Margaret Pridgen, eight years and ten months; Pearl Styles [*sic*], nine years and nine months; and Marion [*sic*] Mercer, 11 years and one month" (May 20).

When Lewis asked him what all those statistics could mean, he answered, "In my opinion, an individual with such mental development would not realize the difference between right and wrong, but would only know that certain things had been indicated to them as right or wrong." In other words, a child of the mental ages he described would have been told that starting a fire was wrong but would not have internalized it—that is, it would be only a fact to her. She would not experience the fear of being caught or the anticipation of the guilt that would follow. In fact she might not feel guilty afterward, having no real sense that setting the fire was wrong. The *News and Observer* commented on the strategy of his remark: "It was on these two contentions that Miss Lewis based her brief appeal to the judge, picturing the defendants as children—unfortunate before they were ever taken to the institution."

Phillips then rose from his chair and approached Dr. Crane and asked him how he had come up with the mental ages of the girls. Crane explained the IQ tests and assured Phillips that they were highly respected in his profession. Phillips continued to question Crane about the tests, asking if tests varied and if the results were always the same each time someone took a test in a different environment, under different health conditions, or with different moods. He asked if the stress of being in jail for a capital offense might cause someone to have a lower score. Crane defended his tests vehemently as they were the basis for much of the work he did as director of the Bureau of Mental Health and Hygiene of the State Board of Charities and Public Welfare.

Then Phillips asked if someone could intentionally change her score, that is, answer in a way to appear less intelligent, less mature, more childlike. Crane at first claimed that this could not be done, but he eventually agreed that although it was not probable, it was possible. In effect, he could be fooled by the test taker into believing what she wanted him to believe.

Lewis's next witness was Lottie Mitchem, who in her interview at Lewis's law office had told disturbing tales of the punishments at Samarcand. Slowly and carefully Lewis went back over the first interview with Lottie, with the exception that the judge had made it impossible for Lottie to give testimony on any girls other than the ones on trial. This weakened the testimony greatly because Lewis could not bring up the multitudes of girls who had been punished in various ways, the girls who had tried to commit suicide after their beatings, the girls who had been chased by bloodhounds, and the lasting effects of some of the most extreme cases—all of which Mitchem had firsthand knowledge about. But Mitchem was able to tell the judge about hearing screams and wails coming from the discipline hall because the girl she heard could have been one of the defendants getting whipped. She had, in addition, seen the effects of a whipping on Josephine French: red streaks across her back that turned to bruises in the days that followed.

After Mitchem told her story, Lewis asked her opinion of Samarcand and its administrators, and Lottie repeated what she had said in her earlier interview with Lewis: "I left in part because of the negative way girls are managed there. They are mere children, and they are often bawled out, told how low down they were and where they came from and what they had done on the outside. Once, a dog story was read to them and then Miss McNaughton's [*sic*] dog—who is a school mascot—was held up by someone, and the girls were asked if they did not wish they were as good as the dog." On the cross-examination Phillips did his best to discredit her stories, asking if she had ever seen a whipping personally or if she knew why the girls were being whipped. Mitchem had to say "no" to these things, but she held firm in her opinion of the harsh punishments, reiterating that she had heard screams and seen more than a few girls with red welts on their backs and legs.

Lewis's third witness for the defense was Georgia Piland, who had been a foods teacher at Samarcand for just three months in the winter of 1930–31. She recounted that she had started working at Samarcand in October 1930 and on her first day was introduced to MacNaughton in the yard, but MacNaughton had ignored her because she was getting a burr out of her dog's mouth. Piland was then sent to the main building, where she asked Miss Stott when she would meet with Miss MacNaughton and find out what she was to do. Stott replied that it might be weeks before MacNaughton decided to speak to her. She learned about her duties instead from some of the student counselors and girls at the school. She was frustrated by the lack of specific instructions and rules and never knowing if she was satisfactory in her job.

When Lewis asked about the conditions at Samarcand and the punishments she had seen, Piland described the unsanitary conditions at the hospital and the fact that diseased girls shared quarters with healthy ones. During this era venereal diseases were believed to be passed by casual contact, and about 30 percent of girls admitted to Samarcand tested positive for venereal disease. On cross-examination Phillips was able to get Piland to admit that each new girl to the institution was kept in the hospital for two weeks before joining the general population, but Piland argued that this was not long enough.

With her next witness, Viola Sistare, Lewis began much the same way as she had with her other witnesses: by asking what role she played at Samarcand and how long she had worked there. Sistare stated that she arrived at the beginning of July 1930 and stayed seven months, serving in the capacity of nurse. Sistare testified much as Piland had, saying that the accommodations for the girls were not proper and that the sanitation was poor. Many of the beds were broken and propped up on chairs and blocks of wood, there were not nearly enough sheets and neither pillowcases nor pillows, and there were no gowns, so sometimes the girls were forced to lie on blankets in just their underwear. For six months, she claimed, she was furnished with neither toothpaste nor toothbrushes. Girls and nurses were forced to sit on the beds because there was no furniture; she said that she had never had a chair during her term at Samarcand.

She also mentioned that the girls having gonorrhea or syphilis were not quarantined from the others. Once they were treated, they were turned loose to infect the rest of the student body, she believed. She claimed that she could show records of girls who had come to Samarcand with negative reports for both syphilis and gonorrhea but then tested positive for one or the other after having been incarcerated at Samarcand for a time.

If permitted, she could have testified to the harsh treatment of many of the girls who had injuries she was then called upon to treat. In her letter to Lewis, she told of a child who came to her in July with her buttocks and upper limbs badly bruised and with large welts. Sistare maintained that she had no desire to interfere with the discipline of the school but felt that if a child found it difficult to walk and was unable to sit, she had better treat the child, so she gave her some "ungentine" and sent her back to her cottage.

In the fall on her day off, one of the younger children came crying to the hospital and asked to see her alone. She went into the operating room with her, where the child showed Sistare her buttocks and legs, which were covered with deep ruts and dried blood. The child was unable to sit down and was predictably a bit hysterical. Knowing that region of the body is easily infected, she cleansed and bathed the child and applied Unguentine ointment and sent her to the hospital ward to stay the night. The child remained there overnight, and her condition was much improved when Sistare saw her the next morning. At about two o'clock the next afternoon, MacNaughton came to the hospital and in no uncertain terms "laid [Sistare] low" for having treated the child. MacNaughton also accused her, in front of girls and staff members, of having spread the report of the child's condition all over the institution.

In her letter Sistare asserted, "Every day my intelligence was questioned, and I received many notes concerning my handling of the children and much unnecessary advice contrary to my better judgment. I had all power of using my professional reason for the girls taken from me to such an extent that I felt myself to be utterly useless and so resigned."

However, these stories and statements went untold in Judge Schenck's courtroom because they did not directly deal with any of the fourteen girls on trial. Lewis had to rely on the few stories she could tell. One newspaper report stated that the "defense also attempted to prove that in the case of some floggings hospital treatment had been necessary. The nearest testimony defense counsel could secure was that she had 'heard' of cases which required infirmary treatment from Miss Stott, secretary to Miss Agnes B. McNaughton [*sic*]" (*News and Observer,* May 21). With these former employees of

Samarcand, Lewis also "sought to bring out the fact that the turn-over of teachers at Samarcand is enormous and that many of them resigned in protest against conditions there. Judge Schenck, who was sitting as jury as well as judge, ruled the defense out of order on this point, however, and no testimony was brought out beyond the fact that four teachers had left within a month of the firing of the buildings." On cross-examination Phillips was able to force Sistare to reiterate that the girls were quarantined for two weeks. That was his only point.

Lewis's next move was to have eight girls testify. She hoped to show the judge that these were indeed children whose unfortunate beginnings had led to their problems. She wanted him to understand that although the girls had pleaded guilty, they were victims of their home lives, their parents, their poverty, and the system that would send them to Samarcand, where they were made victims yet again. Only their individual stories could accomplish this. She had chosen the eight girls who might most make that characterization solid—the eight with stories most likely to make the judge feel compassion and pity.

First she called Margaret Abernethy because her story, out of all those Lewis had heard, created the most sympathy. This girl was a victim in many different ways. Although Margaret was sixteen years old, she could have passed for several years younger. Lewis's notes described her as pale and petite with wispy blond hair framing a face that had obviously suffered from acne. Lewis asked her to tell about her home life before she went to Samarcand, so Margaret told of living in Kinston with her father. Her mother was dead. She had been committed to Samarcand in December 1928 because of her father's mistreatment of her. The truth is that her father committed incest several times every week, and only when he was caught red-handed was he sent to the state penitentiary. Her stepmother, humiliated by the events, did not want her, and Margaret was sent to Samarcand.

Abernethy went on to testify that she had been whipped four times. She had been forced to lie on her stomach while several teachers took turns beating her. Two of the whippings were for trying to run away, one was for being rude to a teacher, and the fourth was for an offense of which she was unaware. In addition she was locked for three months in the discipline cottage, Chamberlain Hall. She admitted to confessing to Miss Stott about her part in the fires and explained that she did it to get out of Samarcand. Under his short cross-examination, Phillips merely asked her if she knew that her whippings were earned—that she had broken rules—and she admitted that she knew she had for the most part, although she was not clear on what those rules were exactly.

The stories continued as Lewis proceeded with her parade of girls on the stand, each one telling her own tale as well as about her treatment at Samarcand. Josephine French, from a small town called Haw River about halfway between Greensboro and Raleigh, had lived with her mother before being sent to Samarcand. Her father had abandoned her, her sister, and two brothers when Josephine was just three. Now she was fifteen. One thing that set her apart from the other girls was that she attended school regularly until the seventh grade, when she dropped out to work at the hosiery mill where her mother worked. Josephine was sent to Samarcand the October before the fires because her mother had seen that she was popular with boys and so dubbed her "immoral and disobedient." In fact, Josephine confessed, she had started having sex with boys about a year before she entered Samarcand, the first time with a sailor who was nineteen. After that, she had admitted to Lewis, she had run around with boys quite often because there was "nothing else to do in Haw River."

She went on to describe her own two whippings with "great big sticks." She also explained that she was generally locked in her room because she had attempted to run away once, and so she had not been involved in any of the fires. When asked why she confessed to a crime she did not commit, she answered the same way many of the girls did: in order to get out of Samarcand (*Southern Pines Pilot,* May 22).

Pearl Stiles, the fifteen-year-old girl who was accused of starting the first fire in Bickett Hall, grew up in Canton, a small mountain town just west of Asheville and almost at the Tennessee line. Her parents were both alive with five children in the family. Her father tried to farm, but the work was hard in the mountains, so most of the time he ran bootleg liquor through the hills to other small towns. When he was home, Pearl had claimed, he was mean and drunk and often hit her mother. Her mother, she admitted, had questionable morals and earned money by "doing favors" for men. Sent to school when she was nine, Pearl attended only once in a while because she had been sick so often with various ailments.

Her parents sent her to Samarcand, she claimed in court, so she could attend school, but Lewis knew that her records at Samarcand showed a different story: like most of the other girls there, she was suspected of immoral conduct. When Lewis had interviewed Pearl earlier, she had asked about the note citing immorality in her records. Pearl had answered, "They put that in everyone's records. I don't know why except maybe they don't believe us." Or perhaps officials just assumed that because she was a poor, white, teenage girl, she would do whatever she had to do for self-benefit.

Pearl had been whipped only once, she had told Lewis, with a leather strap. At the time of the fire, since she was the only one of the defendants who lived in Bickett Hall, that fire was blamed completely on her. Although Pearl had never confessed to it, she said, she had been sent to jail solely on the word of Hilda Godley—one of the witnesses for the prosecution—who claimed Pearl had told her of her involvement.

Lewis's next witness, Ollie Harding, was the youngest of seven children in a family that had lived originally in Washington, D.C., before moving to North Carolina. Ollie, seventeen years old, was one of the oldest of the defendants. She had little education, having dropped out of school to work in a ten-cent store to help support the younger children after her mother died of cancer. Ollie had been sent to Samarcand by her father for "running around" and for "all kinds of delinquency," according to the official records at the school. Her father had since died an alcohol-related death while Ollie was at Samarcand.

Ollie claimed that she was whipped with a hickory stick once for passing a letter to a girl who was locked in her room. Like the other girls, she hated Samarcand and was willing to do anything to get away—even if it meant going to jail. "They didn't treat me right," she testified, as she had claimed in her earlier interview. "They would beat me and lock me up for nothing at all." She claimed to know nothing about the fire in Bickett but was there when the first Chamberlain fire was set, "even though I didn't set it," she remarked. Regarding the second fire in Chamberlain, she explained, "I heard some of the girls say that Margaret Pridgen said that she was going to set it on fire. I wasn't there. I was in bed."

Lewis continued with her witnesses. She called Edna Clark, who told of her three whippings at the hands of the women who ran Samarcand. Marian Mercer told of her dead father and her eventual promiscuity working in her mother's brothel. Dolores Seawell, with her shorn hair, told her story of being whipped with a strap that left blisters on her backside—a punishment for speaking rudely to a teacher. She ran away after that beating, trying to get to any place where they would not beat her for speaking her mind. After she was dragged back, her hair was cut to the scalp as punishment.

Lewis then called to the stand Rosa Mull, the youngest and smallest of the defendants. Rosa's father was a farmer in Rutherfordton, and her mother was in the Western State Hospital for the Insane at Morganton. Forced to take care of a younger sister and two brothers and suffering greatly from poverty, Rosa had not been able to attend school consistently and in desperation had run away. After this happened several times, her father sent her to Samarcand. Her running away continued at the school; once those in charge there sent bloodhounds after her.

As young as she was, Rosa was no angel. Lewis knew that she had a history with men and had begun having sexual relations more than a year before entering Samarcand. She also knew that after one of the times Rosa had run away from Samarcand, the authorities had found her living with a twenty-three-year-old man, but of course Lewis would have stayed far away from that line of questioning.

Fortunately, Phillips stayed away from the girls' sexual histories as well. The cross-examination of each girl was short and uniform. The prosecutor gently pushed each girl until she confessed that her punishments had been for breaking the rules—in essence, that the whippings were deserved because the girls had done something they knew they should not have done. He did not address the severity of the punishments. As to their lives before Samarcand, he questioned them only until he was able to get most of them to admit that their parents or guardians had had a hard time controlling them and that the reason they were sent to Samarcand was because no one knew what else to do with them. Most of them admitted as well that they had tried to run away either from home or from Samarcand, and one admitted to returning with a knife in order to help others escape. Phillips's focus was simple: make the girls admit they had been delinquent, avoiding the question of whether their punishments fit their crimes.

After Lewis ended her defense, Phillips recalled one witness, Estelle Stott, who was no doubt angered by having to listen to each girl disparage Samarcand and the strict order to which she subscribed. Her own reputation had been put on trial as well. Phillips's questions, though, were about only one thing: the lack of proper bedding for girls in the discipline hall. When he asked Stott to explain why the girls in Chamberlain Hall often did not have bedding, she answered that girls had often been known to make escapes from the upper bedrooms by using their sheets to climb down. If the administration felt that a particular girl was at risk for that kind of behavior, her bedding was taken from her; she claimed, however, that this was a rare punishment. When Lewis got a chance to cross-examine Stott, she asked about the vermin the girls had described: the bedbugs and the roaches. Stott admitted it was a problem, but she asserted that the school made every effort to eradicate them. They were persistent creatures, though, she claimed, especially in Chamberlain, which was one of the oldest halls.

Having finally heard everyone testify, Judge Schenck ordered a short break so that the two lawyers could make their final preparations for closings. The long day was coming to an end, but the judge wanted everything finished so that he could have the night to deliberate. The longer this trial continued, the more press it would get and the more weighty his decision would seem. Better to press on and get it done. After conversing for a few minutes with George McNeill, Lewis gathered up her notes and moved to a quiet room. For thirty minutes she pored over her notes once more, putting the final touches on an emotional plea she hoped would sway the judge.

When the judge called everyone back to the courtroom, Lewis was determined. Years of writing her column for the newspaper had prepared her for this moment. She would never be called on again to make such an important speech to sway opinion. Later reports of the day would describe Lewis's speech as the "emotional high point" of the trial, and for years her closing argument was held up as an example of the best of what a lawyer can accomplish in a final speech. Lewis claimed later that it was the best speech she had ever given.

Solicitor Phillips would make his closing argument first. He began by defending Samarcand as the best of what such an institution could be. He praised its organization, its mission, and its record of accomplishments in retraining young girls who had been troubled. He even quoted from Lewis's article from years back that claimed the success of Samarcand could be directly tied to the administration of Agnes MacNaughton. Then he reiterated his statements at the beginning of the trial: the girls had started the fires; they admitted to doing that; and it was the law's responsibility to punish them for the crime of arson. He ended his short speech by stating that the girls "had violated state law, destroyed state property, and endangered many lives."

Lewis rose slowly to her feet and walked around her table to stand directly in front of the judge. She did not hold notes. After a moment, she began. The *News and Observer* included the entire speech in the May 20 issue:

> "Your Honor, two indictments are brought here today. One, the formal legal indictment brought by the solicitor. The other is less tangible but no less real—against society for the presence of these children in a criminal courtroom.

> "These children—like all other children—are the products of their environment, heredity, and the pressure that society has brought to bear on them. Some of them were born mentally defective; others came from broken homes or from homes where parents were handicapped or missing in one way or another.
>
> "They are the products of subtle forces that have played on them since their birth. It is not a case of black and white, but of many varying shades of gray."
>
> She pointed to the girls.
>
> "These children were wards of the State. The State had said they were not getting the proper discipline at home, and North Carolina undertook to stand in the place of their parents. The State recognized they were problem children, children who had a right to expect discipline based on a sympathetic understanding of their problems."
>
> She dropped her arm and once again faced the judge.
>
> "I am not saying they should not be punished, but I am saying that half-grown girls in a civilized community should not be laid on a whipping carpet—when flogging has been abolished in chain gangs! How can we justify such behavior for our children when adult criminals do not even have to suffer such punishment?
>
> "These children are all young, with their eyes to the future, and I think the state whose wards they were when the crime was committed should give them as great a chance as possible.
>
> "I believe in the final divine tribunal, where they will not be judged guilty."

With this ending, Lewis turned and went back to her seat. Up to this point the girls had remained silent, defiant even, in their demeanor, but the words of Lewis changed that. The *News and Observer* recounted, "As she made a brief plea to the Judge for mercy for the children who were the products of their environment, of forces beyond their control or comprehension, the unconcern and defiance of the youthful defendants melted into tears, while handkerchiefs were also brought into use from behind the prisoners' seats in the packed courtroom."

After a few moments, in order to let the murmurs that ran throughout the room settle down, Judge Schenck announced that he would take the night to consider his decision, which would be delivered the next morning. He banged his gavel, slipped out of his seat, and disappeared through a door behind the stand. People began to rise, stretch, and talk excitedly about the day's proceedings. Reporters pushed their way through the crowd and rushed out the door to write their stories. Most of the journalists predicted leniency on the part of the court. The *News and Observer* reported, "Although direct intimation from the Judge was lacking, prevailing opinion among those who followed the course of the hearing today with its revelations as to the defendants themselves as well as to their treatment at Samarcand, is that Judge Schneck [*sic*] in his decision tomorrow will be inclined sharply toward leniency."

That night the judge probably lay in his bed perplexed and anxious about what he would have to do. The girls had pleaded guilty, so he could not in good conscience turn them loose, and even if he could, where would they go? Many of the girls did not have homes, and the homes that some had were unstable at best. He could not send them back to Samarcand because they would likely repeat what they had done to get away. They were children, some of them, so how could he send them to the state penitentiary with hardened criminals who would, in all probability, make them more criminal-like before they were released—if they did not burn the place down first?

He was faced with a no-win situation.

The next day the courtroom was bursting with people filling every seat and standing along the walls. The sidewalks were full of people who had not arrived early enough to get into the courtroom, but they waited outside, wanting to hear the news as soon as they could. Reporters stood with their pens and pads ready, already writing the description of the buzzing room. Writers from virtually every newspaper in the state and some from out of state awaited the judge's verdict.

The Samarcand girls were not buzzing. For the first time they seemed to realize the gravity of their situation and how this morning would probably change the direction of their lives, although they were uncertain what the change would entail.

When Judge Schenck looked up from his notes, he did not look at the people in the courtroom or the lawyers. He looked directly at the row of girls on trial and spoke to them. The *News and Observer* (May 21) recorded his words: "Some of the doctors think you haven't sense enough to know what I'm saying, but I rather think you have." Every girl looked back intently at the judge, sensing his ultimate authority and lulled by the familiarity and concern in his voice. "Now young women, I want to talk to you. You could have been tried for your lives and sent to the electric chair, but the state did not want to send you to the electric chair. You could be sent to the penitentiary for ten years." He paused. "I do not want to do that. But I am an officer of the law, and so I have to make a hard decision."

The News and Observer ~ May 21st 1931.

ARSON DEFENDANTS AND THEIR COUNSEL

Some of the fourteen Samarcand girls on their way to the Moore county court at Carthage yesterday when twelve of the fourteen were sentenced to the State Prison for indeterminate sentences of eighteen months to five years for burning two buildings at Samarcand are shown above. One of the defendants is quite obviously taking the last final puff of her cigarette before facing the judge for sentence.

At the left is Nell Battle Lewis, Raleigh attorney, who while representing only one of the defendants, assumed the brunt of the defense in a dramatic presentation to the judge. It was Miss Lewis' first major case since she started the practice of law and in it she undertook to show unsatisfactory conditions in the State correctional institution.

Twelve Samarcand Girls Get State Prison Terms

Eighteen Months To 5-Year Indeterminate Sentence Imposed

TWO ARE RELEASED ON SUSPENDED SENTENCES

Girls Transported Immediately To State Prison To Begin Terms

By BESS DAVENPORT THOMPSON
Staff Correspondent.

Carthage, May 20.—State Prison doors today clanged behind 12 girls in their teens, unwanted for the most part by their own families, by society, or by the State's correctional institution, two of whose buildings they were sentenced in Moore County Superior Court here today for burning.

From 18 months to five years was the sentence pronounced by Judge Michael Schenck, who reminded them that the State was stronger than they, that it could and would lock them up—for 18 months if they "behaved," for five years if they did not. And although a psychiatrist had adjudged the four prisoners whom he examined as mental defectives, Judge Schenck told them that he thought they could understand him as he recounted their offenses against society.

They listened attentively—the mental defectives, the daughter of a prostitute, the daughter of an insane mother, the daughter of a man now serving a term for a crime against his own child, the daughter of parents who had died in her infancy, leaving her a piece of unwelcome human driftwood—all listened until the Judge came to the sentence of imprisonment in the State Penitentiary. Then they broke into wailing and sobbing, as violent as most of their demonstrations since they first flashed into public attention last March with the firing of two of the State institution's buildings.

The only other sign of emotion they had shown since the trial got under way yesterday morning came at the close of the day yesterday, and was provoked by the sympathy of Nell Battle Lewis, who had assumed the brunt of defense counsel. As she made a brief plea to the Judge for mercy for the children who were the products of their environment, of forces beyond their control or comprehension, the unconcern and defiance of the youthful defendants melted into tears, while handkerchiefs were also brought into use from behind the prisoners' seats in the packed courtroom.

Two of the 14 girls who submitted pleas of guilty of an attempt to commit arson with the understanding that the Judge could dismiss any individuals against whom the testimony was not sufficient to convict, were given suspended sentences, conditioned on good behavior for five years. Rosa Mull, of Wilmington, 13 years old, and the youngest of the defendants, was placed in the custody of her family, a sentence of two years being suggested in the event she was not of good behavior. Margaret Pridgen, of Waynesville, 15 years old, was given a suspended sentence of from one to three years. Both of her parents are dead, and she will be placed either in the home of a relative or in another home.

As the girls were taken from the courtroom, the same procedure was observed as that of yesterday. A deputy was stationed at the main entrance to the courtroom each time the girls were transferred to or from the room, the deputy being given orders to arrest anyone who attempted to pass through the door, while spectators were ordered to keep their seats until the girls had filed from the court, down the steps and through a cordon of deputy sheriffs and court attaches to the waiting school bus which conveyed them to and from the jail.

When spectators descended from the courtroom today, the 12 sentenced prisoners were already speeding on their way to the State Penitentiary in Raleigh, where they were placed above "Death Row," this wing being the only fireproof one of the prison.

Strangely enough, it is in this community, which is next door to Samarcand and which is itself the scene of jail disturbances while the girls were being held here for trial, that the most sympathy is expressed for them.

"Them girls have already been punished twice over for everything they've done. They've been punished ever since they were born," was part of the comment which went along with the service of filling a gasoline tank and radiator.

"It does look like what they need is help, not punishment," a Court House employe observed to a group on the steps as spectators filed from the courtroom.

"They haven't had a chance for anything else since they were born. They've been headed for the penitentiary all their days, and God help the rest of us because no one stepped in to intervene before it was too late. It is a case of being more sinned against than sinning," a more religious spectator observed.

There were also comments to the contrary to be heard, one to the effect that: "I would have locked 'em up for the full ten years," and "There's no hope for them now. They might as well have been put away for life." But the prevailing sentiment seems to be one of surprise that the sentence was as heavy as it is, and that even the minimum of 18 months in the State Penitentiary will do little toward improving the girls as citizens of the State.

But with the State imposing the penalty prescribed by law for crimes against the commonwealth, and with the prisoners being held at the request of the Governor without visitors for the time being, there remains one other feature of the trial which is likely to be of continued interest

(over)

Newspaper story showing Nell Battle Lewis and the only known photograph of some of the Samarcand Sixteen. Courtesy of the State Archives of North Carolina.

The judge turned his attention specifically to Rosa Mull and ordered her to stand. Rosa stood and managed to look even more childlike than her thirteen years. Pale and wide-eyed, she waited to hear her fate. Judge Schenck announced that Rosa would be given a suspended sentence, putting her in the custody of her family, who were ordered to watch over her and make sure she did not step out of line again. If she behaved for the next two years, he went on, the charges would be completely dropped and she would be free. He asked her if she understood, and she nodded.

Margaret Pridgen's name was called next by the judge. Margaret was the second-youngest defendant, and although she had been accused of being the initial instigator by several of the girls, her age would serve her well. Margaret too, he announced, would receive a suspended sentence. Her father was given custody of her, and if she behaved for three years, the charges would be dropped. Judge Schenck asked if that was clear. Margaret nodded at the judge and sat back down.

"The last twelve of you, please stand," he commanded. By now the girls were probably feeling quite confident and optimistic. They stood and waited, but then the tone of the judge's voice changed, and everyone—especially the girls—sensed it immediately. "This is where my job gets especially difficult," began the judge. "You girls are all old enough to know that what you did was wrong. You know that there are consequences for committing a crime like arson, and I'm sure you were aware that people could have gotten hurt because of your little prank." He went on to remind them that they had been sent to Samarcand because they could not be controlled at home, then declared that after the state had done the best it could for them at Samarcand, they were still unruly and rebellious.

Several of the girls suddenly became emotional, their eyes rimmed with tears ready to overflow. It seemed as though they were faced for the first time with the magnitude of their actions. Several girls began to weep openly. Lewis too sensed the change in the judge's attitude and braced herself for the worst. The two youngest had been set free, but the older girls, as she feared, were not to be so fortunate.

The judge explained that as an officer of the law, he had to send them to prison, and so he imposed the same sentence for all twelve: eighteen months to five years in the state penitentiary, depending on their behavior while behind bars. The judge declared, "You have said you would rather go to jail than be in Samarcand. You are going to get that wish. Your stay in the penitentiary depends entirely upon you. If you want to stay there five years, just go down there and set something on fire. If you want to behave yourself, you can get out in less than two years. That is the force that is going to be used on you and the options of the choice you make." He paused and then added, "The state is strong enough to hold you."

With these final words, the judge banged his gavel, stood up, and disappeared into his chambers. The crowd stood as the judge walked out the door, realizing suddenly that it was all over. Many of the faces showed the stunned reaction nearly everyone felt, Lewis as much as anyone.

The girls were led away toward the outside door, where their bus was waiting to take them directly to the state penitentiary in Raleigh. Many of them looked despondent and wept openly, and one small voice protested, shouting, "You may send me to prison, but I'm going to kill myself!" A few of the girls looked angry and defiant even still. One reporter described their emotional outbreak: "Then they broke into wailing and sobbing, as violent as most of their demonstrations since they first flashed into public attention last March with the firing of two of the State institution's buildings" (*News and Observer,* May 21).

It would be the last time they would be seen in public for five years, and for many of them, it would be the last time anyone would even recognize that they mattered in society. They would be virtually forgotten.

SIX

The twelve sentenced girls were transferred immediately by bus to the state penitentiary in Raleigh and put in fireproof cells just above the death-row inmates. Each girl was put in her own cell at first as a way to discourage plotting among them, but the prison authorities said that if they showed themselves to be disciplined, they would get regular prison liberties and be able to keep company with others. Most of them at least tried to follow the rules, but several of the girls were still defiant. They believed, and perhaps rightly so, that behaving had gotten them nowhere, so why not misbehave?

The girls were probably in a state of shock, never having believed that the judge would sentence them—mere teenagers—to the state prison as if they were adult, hardened criminals. The youngest of them had been spared—Rosa Mull was only thirteen and Margaret Pridgen had just turned fifteen—but three others were also only fifteen although some months older than Margaret, and none was older than eighteen.

The public too was shocked by the outcome. Nothing had led the people to expect anything but leniency. The *News and Observer* reported that "the prevailing sentiment seems to be one of surprise that the sentence was as heavy as it is, and that even the minimum of 18 months in the State Penitentiary will do little toward improving the girls as citizens of the State" (May 21). In the days that followed the trial, there was a flurry of stories in the local newspapers and in some of the national ones. Public opinion varied, but most people were on the side of the girls. Local reporters noticed that although Samarcand—with all of its problems so recently brought to light—was "next door" to Carthage, "it is in this community . . . that the most sympathy is expressed for them" (May 21).

One observer, a Carthage gas station attendant who was interviewed for a story, said, "They've been punished ever since they were born." On the steps of the courthouse, an employee of the state noted, "It looks like what they need is help, not punishment." Another trial attendee remarked,

"They haven't had a chance for anything else since they were born. They've been headed for the penitentiary all their days, and God help the rest of us because no one stepped in to intervene before it was too late. It is a case of being more sinned against than sinned." Yet another looked bleakly into the future: "There's no hope for them now. They might as well have been put away for life." The *News and Observer* showed sympathy for the girls—and accuracy—when it described them as "unwanted for the most part by their own families, by society, or by the State's correctional institution" (May 21).

Not all were so sympathetic to the girls, though. One man told the same reporter that he "would have locked them up for a full ten years."

The day after the trial ended, the *Rocky Mount Telegram* predicted a pessimistic outcome for the girls: "When they have completed their sentences in the state's prison, they will have been completely broken. . . . Eighteen months at the least in a drab, monotonous, colorless prison will not make good citizens out of twelve children." Earlier the writer of the article argued that "the girls sent yesterday to state's prison are only children. Their minds, although they are doubtless warped and weakened by the forces of heredity and environment, are plastic, possible to re-shapen [*sic*]. Criminals do not begin by robbing banks. When they have reached that stage they are generally difficult to deal with and as a rule are rather hopeless."

In a letter to the editor in the *Raleigh Times* published shortly after the trial, one reader took aim at Dr. Crane and the role of psychiatry. The letter writer admitted that the "psychiatrist with such a subject would probably have no difficulty whatever in deciding that his exhibits were either morons in fact or with distinct moronic tendencies" and that—in accordance with the prevailing opinion of the day—"in the great majority of cases a woman or a girl given over to this worst of follies is, and always has been, a mental defective." But the writer questioned whether other factors should have been taken into account when working with such young girls: "What causes a woman to elect promiscuity in youth is a question directly related to the mentality."

A week after the trial, Judge Schenck was applauded in the *Charlotte Observer* for his attending "strictly to business when on the bench" and "retaining the human element which is often considered lacking in many judges." Many were just glad the death penalty had been taken off the table, sure that "the plea bargain rescued the State from what might have proved an embarrassing prospect of executing the girls by electric chair" (May 28).

The fear of criticism and public embarrassment was strong in North Carolina and would lead the state to ignore the girls in the penitentiary for years rather than bring up the story again for scrutiny. In fact, despite good behavior by most of the girls, not one of them would get out in the minimum of eighteen months. All would serve the full five-year term in the cell block just above death row.

When the citizens of Rutherfordton found out that young Rosa Mull had been released to her family, they wired Judge Schenck with simple and cruel words: "We don't want her back here." The judge understood their reluctance to accept her back into the community and their worry that she would return to her old ways of causing trouble and running around town. He wired them back explaining that she was not being simply released but rather had received a suspended sentence dependent on her good behavior. If she misbehaved, he told them, she would be sent immediately to jail.

Since Judge Schenck had put Wilma Owens in the custody of Lewis, she had to find a place for Wilma to go. Wilma's parents were both dead, and her younger siblings were in an orphanage that would not take someone as old as Wilma. Lewis first contacted a detention home in Wake County, near Raleigh, but the authorities there refused to accept her, claiming that "we have no fireproof building, the building itself being a very old wooden structure," so therefore, "it would be unwise to take any outside cases in at this present time, both for the sake of the inmates and property of the county." After trying several other kinds of homes and being turned away for the same reason, Lewis took Wilma to live with Wilma's elderly grandmother in Haywood County in the mountains near Asheville, even though her grandmother was not prepared to supervise a teenage girl. There was simply no other solution.

Lewis received many letters from people who had followed the trial in the newspapers. A minister from Greensboro wrote expressing his admiration for her work in the trial. Even though most of the girls went to jail, he said, he remained optimistic about the effect the trial might have on society: "Perhaps this case may be instrumental in pointing the way to a saner method of dealing with society's recalcitrant members. Taken at its worst this is less the problem of delinquent girls than that of delinquent society." Lewis, less optimistic, wrote back to him on May 24: "I did all I could for these poor girls, but it was not enough to save twelve of them from the Penitentiary, out of which they will come at the experiation [*sic*] of their sentences even more bitter enemies of society than they are now."

Another man pointed out the irony of the situation in his letter to Lewis: "One judge frees criminal bankers for cash, and another, a stranger to . . . Jesus Christ . . . turns a deaf ear upon your logical and eloquent plea in behalf of twelve children wrecked upon the desert we call civilization." He congratulated her for her "kind heart" and "enlightened understanding of society toward its progeny." A friend of Lewis wrote to her and remarked on her "splendid defence [*sic*] and appeal for those unfortunate girls." She thanked Lewis for her "understanding heart" and claimed that "this experience in your profession is but the beginning of a great future, great in its fullest, highest sense."

Another writer, clearly an advocate of eugenics, pointed out what he saw as the genetic inevitability of the girls' behavior: "some . . . are mental defectives, one a daughter of a prostitute, one a daughter of an insane mother, one a daughter of a man now serving a term for a crime against his own child, others who are daughters of parents who died in their infancy." He went on to suggest that the whole problem of the Samarcand girls could have been solved if their mothers and their mothers' mothers had not been allowed to reproduce: "Who made that daughter's mother a prostitute? First answer that: Who contributed to the other mother's insanity? Or what was society doing to avoid by prudent law the birth of that daughter unto an insane mother, to be a curse to herself and that 'noble, innocent' society? What does society hold against the daughter of a pervert father—unless it be first held against society's lack of vigilance two generations ago?" He continued, citing the fourteen states that had laws restricting procreation of the mentally ill or unfit, but he believed they were all ineffectual ones that were "only sop lapped up by dusty, thirsty pigeon-holes, or serving as conscience salve to a careless, weak-kneed and disinterested gang of office-seekers and unthinking followers."

Lewis also received letters from the families of the girls, letters that confirmed her suspicions that the families did not understand how the justice system works. Chloe Stillwell's mother pleaded with Lewis to ask the governor to pardon Chloe. She offered a petition signed by the citizens of her hometown, Kinston, and claimed that she could even get the jailer Austin Smith, from Lumberton, to sign it. Lewis wrote back advising her to wait thirty days before taking any action, adding, "I was distressed that so many received prison sentences. I really think that Choel [*sic*] is one who should have been released, at least under suspended judgment." Virginia Hayes's mother wrote requesting that Lewis visit the governor and ask if he would let Virginia out of prison if she promised to be good. None of this, however, was done, and the girls remained in prison.

EPILOGUE

Repercussions

Eventual good did come from the trial in regard to the prison system and Samarcand in particular, although at first it appeared that nothing positive would follow. On May 30 it was reported that Mrs. J. R. Page, a member of the board of trustees and secretary to the board of Samarcand, was questioned about what would happen regarding the charges made against the administration and its punishment policies. She defended Samarcand's policies in the *News and Observer:*

> "Miss Stott testified," said Mrs. Page, "that only three girls had been whipped and this was not done unmercifully." Mrs. Page added that sometimes a switch and sometimes a strap is used in administering punishment to the girls and that ten to fifteen licks are given.
>
> Asked about the testimony as to bed bugs, Mrs. Page said it was no doubt true there were some bed bugs in the Chamberlain building as this was an old building and it was difficult to keep the insects out, but that it was distinctly not true as to the other buildings. Mrs. Page said she was sure the girls who were placed on the stand at Carthage greatly exaggerated conditions.

Rumors of a cover-up abounded: On May 29 the *Chapel Hill Weekly* reported, "The descriptive term, 'vixens,' applied to them by the *Raleigh Times* is certainly not too severe. But the character of these girls does not excuse in the slightest degree the outrageous conditions at Samarcand revealed in the testimony; and the forecast of a whitewash by the board of charities and public welfare is disappointing." The article went on to quote more from the *Raleigh Times:* "If only a part of the things to which they testified is true, the fact that they are apparently more corrupt than when they entered the institution is easily understandable." The reporter then issued a call to action:

> All of which demands a full and unsparing investigation of the whole Samarcand project. Its purpose is not that of the old-fashioned "reformatory" to which delinquents were sent frankly as punishment by term of imprisonment. It was created, on the other hand, on a wave of pity for the plight of girls of tender years, with the idea that they might thus be rescued, inspired and redeemed. But the whole trend of the testimony heard following the pleas goes to show that the place has been in some measure akin to a jail or a penitentiary in which associations confirm rather than modify the existing fault.

After all, the reporter continued, "Something made these children come to the point of revolt and frenzy. It must have been something extraordinary to have raised such a spirit of rebellion in such a type of girls." The motive and even the competency of the administration also, of course, came under scrutiny. The *Chapel Hill Weekly* warned that it would be hard to find girls to tell the truth because "there are dozens of ways in which a petty tyrant can make more miserable the life of an inmate who tells the truth too freely." The paper suggested instead that statements be taken from "persons of good characters, teachers and nurses, who were recently at Samarcand and no longer have any connection with the institution" because "they possess the necessary knowledge and, at the same time, are in a position not to be penalized for telling the truth."

In the weeks following the trial, the National Commission of Prisons released a statement: "The call today—and never before has it sounded so clearly and so strongly—is for the great forces in the community . . . to [mobilize] . . . so that from the ashes of burning buildings, from the bloodshed and riot of the past year will grow rapidly and surely [a] . . . new and better system."

A similar call to action came from most of the state's newspapers and many state politicians. The day after sentencing, the *Greensboro News* reported, "Enough has been brought out [during the trial] to demand a searching inquiry and corrective steps which will assure youthful delinquents . . . treatment as humane as that accorded hardened convicts." Soon thereafter the *Rocky Mount Telegram* challenged the role of training schools as well as their punishment policies: "Young girls cannot be beaten with sticks and straps, placed in rooms where sleep is difficult because of roaches and be made to believe that the state, that the school or that the officials of the school have even so much as a remote interest in them. Nor have young girls become so monstrous at the age of 16 that it is impossible to at least partially reform them. No one expects Samarcand to produce the flower of womanhood. One does expect that Samarcand will at least instill in its inmates some self-respect, some appreciation for values."

The latter plea was heard by Governor Gardner, who contacted the Board of Trustees of Samarcand and the North Carolina State Board of Charities and Public Welfare and ordered them to launch their own internal investigations into the practices at the school. In her column written just days after the trial ended, Lewis applauded the governor's decision but lamented that it had not happened sooner to help the Samarcand girls.

One investigation had already taken place. On March 31, almost two months before the trial, three members of the State Board of Charities and Public Welfare had visited Samarcand for four days and interviewed staff and inmates, looked through files, and observed the organization and tactics of the school. The next week two more members spent four more days finishing up the inspection at Samarcand. This was followed by several weeks of compiling and analyzing information. In addition institutions were contacted in other states and compared to Samarcand, especially in the area of discipline.

The board eventually concluded after the trial that within the school at the current time there was a "congenial and cooperative spirit among the present staff" and that it was only former employees who had a "disrupting, harmful influence" because they simply were "people who were not fitted at all for work in an institution of this type." The board also decided that the methods of isolating girls with venereal diseases were "in accord with the approved medical practice" delineated in the law. In addition they admitted that about 20 percent of the girls at Samarcand were "incorrigible" but that 80 percent were "salvageable."

Corporal punishment was a major issue since during the trial the witnesses for the defense had relayed such harrowing tales of beatings. Authorities concluded, however, that the floggings were highly exaggerated during the trial and that in reality, "the whippings were not severe, the average number of strokes for each whipping being about ten. The average number of whippings per month was estimated at one. Only light switches were used." Despite these positive conclusions, a sense of unease persisted among board members, leading them to abolish corporal punishment altogether and replace it with isolation in new "thinking rooms." In addition a restricted diet for girls who misbehaved—rather than just bread and water, a diet that would not "impair the health of the girl"—was approved. The board also required that a written record be made of all punishments.

Board members recommended that a woman be hired as assistant superintendent to take charge of all disciplinary matters so that the job would no longer fall on the shoulders of Miss MacNaughton and her ring of followers. Next they mandated that a car be provided to create a way for workers occasionally to escape from the isolation of Samarcand—a move, they hoped, that would retain teachers and other workers for longer periods by making them more content with their situation.

Concerning the girls, the board decided that "no girls should be admitted to this institution because of being 'neglected, dependent, or homeless.'" This presumably would keep girls such as Margaret Abernethy, the incest victim, from being sent to a home for troubled girls. It was recommended that girls, upon entering Samarcand, be given a clear understanding of how long their stay there would be and what behavior would make them eligible for parole. The board hoped that by making these changes, Samarcand could once again be seen as a positive and successful resource for helping troubled white girls in the state of North Carolina.

Lewis felt that the changes made by the State Board of Charities and Public Welfare in 1931 after the trial were not enough. In the weeks following the trial, she wrote to her friend Kate Burr Johnson—a former member of that board—lamenting that most of the negative information about Samarcand had not been exposed at the trial because the judge had not allowed information that did not relate specifically to the defendants. Lewis knew that Miss Stott was the center of the problems at Samarcand, the one who wielded and abused the real power at the school, and was afraid that in the long run everything would be "beautifully whitewashed." She felt that if things did not change more drastically, another "violent outbreak of the inmates" would occur.

Agnes MacNaughton was retained to run Samarcand—which she did until late 1934—despite what many felt was her failing physical and mental health. In 1968, the fiftieth anniversary of the opening of Samarcand, a celebration pamphlet described her as an "able woman" who possessed "remarkable humanity and resourcefulness." No mention was made of the arson and the trial except the information that "two dormitories, Bickett and Chamberlain, burned in the early nineteen thirties and were replaced."

When Agnes MacNaughton left in 1934, she suffered from depression so deeply that she moved to Pine Bluff Sanatorium in Moore County. She died just four years later. After the school was under new leadership, its reputation began to improve, and by 1939 Samarcand was reputed to have the "warm, helpful, kindly heart of a great commonwealth." In 1945 Nell Lewis reviewed the school's progress and concluded that it had become a well-run institution. Boys and African Americans had joined the student body by the 1970s, and the school's new and improved reputation continued until the summer of 2011, when state budget cuts caused the closing of the school, after which the students were released or sent to other institutions. In 2017 the buildings stand vacant, a reminder of recent hard economic times for North Carolina and the rest of the country.

George McNeill continued practicing law, eventually becoming a clerk of the superior court in Moore County. He died in 1946.

Judge Michael Schenck received many letters of both criticism and support after the trial. The Daughters of the American Revolution chapter in Chapel Hill had written to him at the start of the trial pleading for mercy for the "underprivileged members of society, some of whom are mental defectives," and its members were therefore—like many other people—disappointed in the judge's actions. Schenck continued to serve as judge of the superior court until 1934, when he was sworn in as associate justice of the Supreme Court of North Carolina. He served until January 1948 and died later that year.

In the months following the trial, Dr. Harry Crane communicated with Lewis through more than a dozen letters. He was concerned, even angry, that his traveling expenses, a total of $36.65, had not been paid by Moore County, and Lewis spent a good part of the summer working to get his reimbursement, to no avail. In September she paid him out of her own pocket.

Dr. Crane continued serving as psychiatrist to the State Board of Charities and Public Welfare and became one of the state's biggest proponents for the eugenics program. With his colleague R. Eugene Brown, who had written the mission statement for Samarcand in 1917, and a few others, he pushed for the establishment of the Eugenics Board of North Carolina, which was created two years after the Samarcand trial. On August 4, 1935, the Eugenics Board wrote an article outlining the necessities and advantages of eugenic sterilization, especially within state-run schools such as Samarcand, which was listed as "one of the main cooperating institutions" for sterilization.

In the late 1940s the focus of the Eugenics Board changed from mental and physical illness to the sterilization of those living in poverty and those who were illegitimate. In the 1950s the emphasis became welfare recipients, which led to a significant rise in sterilizations of African Americans. When the board was abolished in 1977, over seventy-six hundred North Carolinians had been sterilized, many of them against their will or without their knowledge. Some of the victims were as young as ten. Of those sterilized, 25 percent were listed as mentally ill and 70 percent as mentally deficient. Females accounted for 75 percent of sterilizations.

Only recently in North Carolina have attempts been made to address the wrongs inflicted through this practice and to offer compensation to those victims still living. A task force decided in January 2012 that "each living person sterilized as part of the state's formal eugenics program, which lasted from 1929 to 1974, should receive $50,000," reported the *New York Times* (January 10, 2012). The bill passed the North Carolina House, but the North Carolina Senate refused to take it up. Even though money was designated for sterilization victims in the budget of Governor Pat McCrory, nothing yet has been done, and many doubt that it will.

North Carolina was, however, taking steps to bring to light this shameful part of its history. By 2013, according to the *Independent Weekly* (Durham) on October 9, 2013, the state was including information about the eugenics movement in its American history high school course as well as in eighth grade social studies classes. In addition a historical marker was put near where the Eugenics Board met:

EUGENICS BOARD
State action led to the
sterilization by choice or
coercion of over 7,600
people, 1933–1973. Met
after 1939 one block E.

The shame resulting from this use of eugenics theory has been tangible in North Carolina and the rest of the world. The issue has been discussed in the news, on television shows, and in the courts. The idea of sterilizing persons without their consent in order to keep the population pure seems unthinkable in today's world. One scholar has written,

> A British critic observed that sterilization laws would have stopped Queen Victoria from having children, for she was "heterozygous for hemophilia." According to Langdon-Davies, "History is packed with examples where eugenic interference would have impoverished the world beyond repair." The biologist Raymond Pearl even quantified

> the potential calamity, estimating that "95 percent of the greatest philosophers, poets, and scientific men that have actually appeared during the history of our race would never have been born" had eugenics policies been in force. (Chamberlain 182)

In 1931, however, a small group of people had made the decision that poor, young, white girls such as the Samarcand Sixteen should be separated from society, first at Samarcand and next in prison. Genetics had marked these girls as cacogenic—that is, breeders of a weak race—and no matter what they would do in their lives, they would not be able to overcome what society had deemed a defect.

Although many people praised Nell Lewis for her brave defense of the girls—as daring and bold as any lawyer they had seen—she also received a great deal of criticism from her own social class for defending poor and uneducated girls. She wrote in a letter to a friend, "I have been sharply criticized for my connection with this case, but I am thoroughly satisfied about it in my own mind." She remarked, "The State Board of Public Welfare has construed my defense of these girls . . . as an attack on the Board. I am now regarded by former allies as an enemy of the welfare work." Her defense of the girls also caused a rift in the ranks of feminists. Since so many members of the board were women and many females were involved with Samarcand, women in general were more invested in the case, and some felt that Lewis's motivation for taking the case was fame. In 1953, though, she said that while defending the girls, she "saw North Carolina at its worst" and that "outraged by their situation, their defense was something I could really get my teeth into—and my heart."

Lewis had every intention of fighting to get the girls free from prison as soon as possible by filing for appeals. She visited the girls in prison several times in the weeks following the verdict. The first time, on May 26, she was turned away by the warden, who said the girls needed more time to settle in. Later she visited them and found all but four behaving well in hopes of being released. Only Dolores Seawell, Virginia Hayes, Josephine French, and Bertha Hall continued to make trouble whenever they could, and Lewis tried several times to talk them into controlling their rage. Anger and defiance ate at their souls, though, and the girls did not seem to care about being the compliant prisoners everyone wanted them to be.

With the encouragement of the public, Lewis attempted to get schooling added to the girls' daily schedule, but although the warden said he would look into it—if all the girls learned to behave—the classes were never created. Public attention and interest dissipated in the months following the trial, and the girls were generally forgotten, left to spend five years of their youth in jail.

For a while, though, individuals and organizations continued to send letters to Lewis. Some expressed their desire to help the girls, but mainly they offered condolences and expressed helplessness with a system that would punish children so severely. One man wrote about the outcome: "We rather pay judges to add bitterness to a story already sordid, and sorrow and misery to an unfortunate already a millstone to his own neck and a land-mark of pity in the sight of God." Others commended Lewis for her efforts, calling her work "noble."

Soon after the Samarcand trial, Nell Battle Lewis became ill with a mysterious disease that gave her great pain in her mouth. While she wanted to follow up on the case, she was unable to do so, instead spending many months running back and forth to Richmond, Virginia, to see experts who might cure her. She had surgery just a month after the trial to remove part of an infected jawbone, but the surgery had little effect on the pain that dogged her and baffled her doctors. In July of that year she wrote to Chloe Stillwell's family that she was not well and would not be able to attend to her law business regularly. Regretfully, she said, "I think I shall have to ask you to put the matter of Chloe's pardon or parole in the hands of some other lawyer."

Like Agnes MacNaughton, Lewis suffered a bout of depression as 1931 progressed, probably a combination of her unresolved illness, her new financial problems, as the Great Depression was eating away at her inheritance, and what she saw as the negative outcome for twelve of the sixteen girls at the trial. By the end of the year she had voluntarily entered Tucker Sanatorium, where she rested and recovered until the next April. She returned to writing her column in May 1932, and readers—not knowing why her column had been missing for a year—were unable to tell from her once-again forceful writing that she had struggled so intensely for the past twelve months.

This was the beginning of the end of Lewis's legal career, however. She never again tried a case and eventually gave up her law office. She suffered several more bouts of depression and had subsequent sojourns at Tucker Sanatorium, but she always rallied, returned home, and resumed her journalistic work. She continued to write her column "Incidentally" for the *News and Observer,* making a reputation for herself as a voice for the victim and the underdog. To her brothers' credit, despite her conflicts with them, they supported her throughout her battles with despondency.

Nell Battle Lewis in her later years. Courtesy of the State Archives of North Carolina.

As she grew older, she became increasingly conservative in her political positions, something her brothers applauded. She renounced many of her earlier liberal positions on freedom of thought and social reform, even attacking previous allies such as the former president of the University of North Carolina, Frank Porter Graham. She used her column to rail against communism and became so combative that she was nicknamed "Battling Nell." She went so far as to apologize in the *Gastonia Gazette* for her actions on the part of labor in the 1929 strike in Gastonia. The newspaper described her words as "a confession of how very wrong she was . . . in upholding what she thought were the rights of down trodden labor, when she was beating the drums for one of the meanest bunch of Communists in the U.S." (July 7, 1947). However, she never changed her opinions about prison reform, women's rights, and the rights of the mentally ill. She continued to fight for these causes in her column and in articles she wrote for professional journals.

From 1937 to 1944 and again briefly in 1954, in addition to writing her newspaper columns, Lewis taught English and Bible studies at St. Mary's College, the private school across the street from her home that she had attended as a young girl. On June 21, 1953, in her column "Incidentally," she reflected on the Samarcand girls in relation to the girls she had taught daily at St. Mary's and concluded that such a rebellion would have taken place even at St. Mary's if conditions had been what they were at Samarcand.

In her columns she continued to promote higher education for women and the improvement of rape laws, and she lobbied for property rights for women. She worked to improve the conditions of women in the workplace, at schools, in prisons, and in homes. She even attacked churches for their subservient expectations for women. In an article published fifteen years after the trial, she reflected on the trial and her closing argument: "I felt that speech absolutely from the heart. I knew those girls weren't to blame. There wasn't a normal one among them, and, too, they were victims of their environment. My address consisted of a terrific indictment of society. In spite of the fact that I didn't get but four of the girls off, I feel that my work in that case was worthwhile" (*News and Observer,* September 1, 1946).

During the years following the trial, she was unable to keep up with the Samarcand girls in their prison stays. In one of her columns more than twenty years later, in 1953, Lewis reflected on her role in the Samarcand arson trial as "one of the most interesting experiences" of her life. There she described Agnes MacNaughton as having "rapidly failing mental health" so that "control had passed into the hands of a cruel subordinate"—that is, Estelle Stott. Lewis justified the girls' revolt and subsequent burning of buildings by blaming the capricious administration that could force a girl to lie on the floor to be "lashed with a leather strap two inches wide." She went on: "I thought to myself: Society has indicted these children for a crime punishable by death, whereas, actually, they should indict society for the high crime of having so largely made them what they are. The State permits the existence of the evil environments from which they come, environments of poverty and depravity, where the mother often is a prostitute, where incest with the father is common. What can you expect!"

She lamented that she had been able to get only four of the girls set free but was proud, at least, that she had been able to get the indictment changed to a lesser charge that did not end with execution. In a June 21, 1953, column, she wrote, "I wanted to keep up with the twelve thus sentenced, but I got sick and couldn't. I know the fate of only one of the sixteen, one of the four who got off. She killed herself." Wilma Owens had committed suicide in 1933. She had been one of the two girls not prosecuted, but somehow she had felt that life was not worth living and so had drunk Lysol (McLaurin and Russell 236).

In 1948 Lewis left the *News and Observer* and moved to the *Raleigh Times,* where she became associate editor, the first woman in North Carolina to reach that position and the highest spot in journalism any woman had yet attained in the state. Praise came in from newspapers all over the state: Sanford Martin, editor of the *Winston-Salem Sentinel,* wrote on July 3, "We know of no one better fitted . . . to establish a precedent in this field than this able teacher-writer whose philosophy has mellowed with the years, and whose liberalism, while tinged now with a sense of realism unknown to the zealous young 'radical' of some twenty-odd years ago, is still a true and abiding thing." She continued to expose injustice in the state through the *Raleigh Times* for another eight years. On the night of November 26, 1956, she drove home from work, stepped out of her car, and collapsed in the front yard, the victim of a heart attack.

Little is known about the Samarcand girls except that they were not released early and all twelve served their full five years. It is possible that their experiences turned rebellious young girls—at least eight of whom Lewis was sure were completely innocent—into embittered women. Since some of them had perhaps been sterilized as part of the eugenics program, they would have had no progeny to stand for them in society. They have truly been erased from history, and the story of the arson and the subsequent trial is just a footnote in North Carolina's story.

Earlier researchers managed to track down Margaret Pridgen, perhaps the instigator of the fires at Samarcand. Margaret was one of the two girls not sent to prison but rather given probation. It is significant that although she married, she never had a child even though she desperately wanted one. In her notes Lewis wrote that Margaret had had an "appendectomy." Was Margaret another victim of sterilization? We will never know for sure, but the clues seem to point that way. Margaret died at the age of sixty-three in 1979 at Oak Manor Nursing Home in Kinston (McLaurin and Russell 236–37).

Rosa Mull, the other girl given probation, was unable to uphold the terms of her probation. The town that did not want her back watched her closely and noted every deviation from good behavior. Only three months after the trial, Rosa was sent to the penitentiary to serve a two-year sentence; she was a victim of her community's "dread of her influence" (McLaurin and Russell 238).

In retrospect, many historians and sociologists have considered the trial from other angles. Some northerners smiled wryly and said, "That's the South for you," feeling that the trial was yet another witness to the brutality that occurred regularly below the Mason-Dixon line. But in some ways the verdict validated the reputation of the New South as it attempted to move away from the vigilantism that had marked many of the Jim Crow years. The death penalty, after all, had been removed as a possibility.

Since the late nineteenth century, the South had been trying to overcome the social, political, and economic problems brought on by the Civil War and its aftermath, and the educated and powerful in North Carolina were fearful of being embarrassed in the eyes of outsiders. The Civil War had devastated the South and imbued it with a sense of inferiority.

In the decade of the 1920s southerners were working mightily to overcome outsiders' images of the South as barbaric and uncivilized, images that had resulted partly from reports of lynchings, which had reached their peak between 1890 and 1930. Just a few months before the Samarcand fires, a black man named Oliver Moore was dragged from the Edgecombe County Jail in Tarboro, North Carolina, driven away, and lynched by a mob. While this might have gone unnoticed in earlier years, the South was beginning to worry so much about its backward reputation that the governor became involved and declared that the lynchers would be punished. Despite his promise, however, the investigation was cursory and no arrests were made. The Samarcand Sixteen trial offered an opportunity to show the rest of the country—and the world—that southerners had a new identity and were no longer backward and undisciplined, and that in the South the legal system would triumph and justice would be served.

Judge Schenck was especially aware of the reputation he was trying to refute. He knew that if he released the girls without any punishment, it would suggest that the system was biased—that if you were female, young, and white you had a better chance of beating the system than if you were black, older, and male. Annette Louise Bickford has explained: "Given the mass destruction of state property and the girls' chequered sexual histories, this ruling might be considered a political act of cool rationality. Schenck exercised rule of law to the extent that the defendants were brought to trial and punished. Partial mercy signified the ruling as a political act, whereby discretion allowed for the legitimate attenuation of a punishment that would have seemed cruel by the national mores of the time, and disadvantageous from the perspective of a region of Americans wishing to present a 'civilised' countenance for the nation and the world at large" (455).

In effect, the act of convicting them rather than letting them return to their homes—those who had them—was showing a respect for the law that the South needed the rest of the country to see. However, Schenck did not send them to the electric chair, for that would have reinforced the image of the South as barbaric, as it would have "made North Carolina's criminal justice system seem exceptionally cruel by the national standards of the time" (Bickford 438). Bickford concluded that the Samarcand trial became a "show trial" illustrating to the rest of the country and the world that North Carolina's national identity aligned itself with the more civilized world, and that Judge Schenck's "decision was informed by a series of interconnected ideas about sexuality, national danger, 'civilisation' and 'race'" (456).

Much of the public would disagree with Judge Schenck, believing that the girls were given a punishment far beyond what they deserved and that trying them as adults rather than as children in juvenile court was a mistake. In any case, whether not putting the girls on trial for their lives showed leniency or the punishment was too severe for the crime, North Carolinians seemed to decide that it was better to forget the whole affair and move forward. Few people in Carthage—whether local citizens or court officials—seemed to remember the trial and the temporary notoriety it brought Moore County, and Samarcand officials swept the whole incident under the rug, preferring, understandably, to focus on the otherwise positive history of the school. When Moore County needed more storage space, they burned old records, including those of the Samarcand trial.

The convenience of forgetting, however, has one major flaw: the Samarcand Sixteen. Born on the lowest rung of the socioeconomic ladder, the girls were given no hand up, no incentive to better themselves. Instead they were beaten—literally—down. As mere children, they were held to the standards of adult behavior and punished for their acts of civil disobedience—a right on which America was founded. In the end they were put away from the rest of society and forgotten as human refuse—perhaps the greatest crime of all.

Works Cited

Bickford, Annette Louise. "Imperial Modernity, National Identity and Capital Punishment in the Samarcand Arson Case, 1931." *Nations and Nationalism* 13.3 (2007): 437–60.

Boggs, Bell. "Extraordinary Justice." *Independent Weekly* (Durham), October 9, 2013, 20–22.

Brietz, Margaret C. "Case Studies of Delinquent Girls in North Carolina." Master's thesis. University of North Carolina at Chapel Hill, 1927.

Brown, R. Eugene. "Eugenical Sterilization in North Carolina." Box PC 255.28, folder 3. North Carolina Archives, Raleigh.

Cahn, Susan K. *Sexual Reckonings: Southern Girls in a Troubling Age.* Cambridge, Mass.: Harvard University Press, 2007.

Chamberlain, Ava. *The Notorious Elizabeth Tuttle: Marriage, Murder, and Madness in the Family of Jonathan Edwards.* New York: New York University Press, 2012.

Currell, Susan, and Christina Cogdell, eds. *Popular Eugenics: National Efficiency and American Mass Culture in the 1930s.* Athens: Ohio University Press, 2006.

Darrow, Clarence. "The Edwardses and the Jukeses." *American Mercury* (October 1925): 147–57.

Dugdale, R. L. *The Jukes: A Study in Crime, Pauperism, Disease and Heredity.* New York: Putnam, 1895.

Fernald, Walter. "Care of the Feeble-minded." In *Proceedings of the National Conference on Charities and Correction.* Columbus, Ohio: Press of Fred. J. Heer, 1904.

Galton, Francis. *Essays on Eugenics.* London: Eugenics Education Society, 1909.

Hooten, Earnest. *Crime and the Man.* 1939. Reprint, New York: Greenwood, 1968.

Kuhl, Stefan. *For the Betterment of the Race: The Rise and Fall of the International Movement for Eugenics and Racial Hygiene.* Trans. Lawrence Schofer. New York: Palgrave Macmillan, 2013.

Larson, Edward J. *Sex, Race, and Science: Eugenics in the Deep South.* Baltimore: Johns Hopkins University Press, 1995.

Leidholdt, Alexander S. *Battling Nell: The Life of Southern Journalist Cornelia Battle Lewis, 1983–1956.* Baton Rouge: Louisiana State University Press, 2009.

Lewis, Nell Battle. Papers. State Archives of North Carolina, Raleigh. Contained here are many newspaper articles including but not limited to the *News and Observer, Elizabeth City Daily Advance, Charlotte Observer, Moore County News,*

Greensboro News, Chapel Hill Weekly, Rocky Mount Telegram, High Point Enterprise, Raleigh Times, and *Southern Pines Pilot;* Lewis's personal notes on the defendants and their families; notes from interviews; letters to and from interested parties; articles on related subjects; trial notes, including sources for Lewis's opening and closing arguments; and information on Samarcand Manor.

McLaurin, Melton, and Anne Russell. *The Wayward Girls of Samarcand: A True Story of the American South.* Wilmington, N.C.: Bradley Creek, 2012.

Mencken, H. L. "The Sahara of the Bozart." In *H. L. Mencken: Prejudices, First, Second, and Third Series.* New York: Library of America, 2010.

———. "Utopia by Sterilization." *Population Review* 4.1 (1960): 17–22.

O'Brien, Gerald V. *Framing the Moron: The Social Construction of Feeble-Mindedness in the American Eugenic Era.* Manchester: Manchester University Press, 2013.

Pyron, Darden Asbury. "Nell Battle Lewis and the 'New Southern Woman.'" In *Perspectives on the American South: An Annual Review of Society, Politics and Culture,* vol. 3, ed. James C. Cobb and Charles R. Wilson, 63–84. New York: Gordon and Breach, 1985.

Wertheimer, John. "Escape of the Match-Strikers: The Samarcand Arson Case of 1931." In *Law and Society in the South: A History of North Carolina Court Cases.* Lexington: University Press of Kentucky, 2009.

Wiggam, Albert. *The Fruit of the Family Tree.* Indianapolis: Bobbs-Merrill, 1926.

Woodside, Moya. "Sterilization and Social Welfare: A Study of Current Development in North Carolina." *Eugenics Review* 40.4 (1949).

———. *Sterilization in North Carolina: A Sociological and Psychological Study.* Chapel Hill: University of North Carolina Press, 1950.

Woodward, Julian L. "The Field of Population Quality." *Social Forces* 17.1 (1938): 468.

Index

About the Author

BARBARA BENNETT is an associate professor of English at North Carolina State University. She is the author of five books, including *Understanding Jill McCorkle,* published by the University of South Carolina Press, and *Soul of a Lion.*